se return this book on or before the last date
stamped below.

Tourism Reassessed

D0452342

Tourism Reassessed
Blight or blessing?

Frances Brown

DC029552
NEWCASTLE-UNDER-LYME
COLLEGE LEARNING
RESOURCES
338. 4791

**BUTTERWORTH
HEINEMANN**

OXFORD   AMSTERDAM   BOSTON   LONDON   NEW YORK   PARIS
SAN DIEGO   SAN FRANCISCO   SINGAPORE   SYDNEY   TOKYO

Butterworth-Heinemann
An imprint of Elsevier Science
Linacre House, Jordan Hill, Oxford OX2 8DP
225 Wildwood Avenue, Woburn MA 01801-2041

First published 1998
Reprinted 2000
Transferred to digital printing 2002

Copyright © 1998, Frances Brown. All rights reserved

The right of Frances Brown to be identified as the author
of this work has been asserted in accordance with the
Copyright, Designs and Patents Act 1988

No part of this publication may be reproduced in any material form (including
photocopying or storing in any medium by electronic means and whether
or not transiently or incidentally to some other use of this publication) without
the written permission of the copyright holder except in accordance with the
provisions of the Copyright, Designs and Patents Act 1988 or under the terms of
a licence issued by the Copyright Licensing Agency Ltd, 90 Tottenham Court Road,
London, England W1T 4LP. Applications for the copyright holder's written
permission to reproduce any part of this publication should be addressed
to the publisher

British Library Cataloguing in Publication Data
A catalogue record for this book is available from the British Library

ISBN 0 7506 4705 1

For information on all Butterworth-Heinemann Publications
visit our website at www.bh.com

NEWCASTLE-UNDER-LYME
COLLEGE LEARNING
RESOURCES

Contents

NEWCASTLE-UNDER-LYME
COLLEGE LEARNING
RESOURCES

Preface

It is twenty-five years since, with his book *Tourism: Blessing or Blight?*, Sir George Young first alerted the world to the size and significance of the tourism industry and to its sometimes negative social and environmental impacts. Even its economic benefits, he argued, were not always as great or as appropriate as tourism's supporters believed.

Since that time the industry has grown ever larger – and the indications are that it will continue to do so – as has the number of critiques it has attracted. Highlighting the negative side of tourism has become a commonplace; that it is at best a mixed blessing almost received wisdom. What has struck me when reading about tourism (and as Editor of *Tourism Management* between 1987 and 1996 I found myself reading about it a great deal) is how so much material failed to place tourism within the wider context of the global political economy. Yet tourism does not take place within a vacuum: it is part of international relations and the form its impacts take has to be seen as resulting from the structure of those relations.

This book is an attempt to locate tourism within the current global political economy and to investigate its effects (on both hosts and tourists) in this context. I have approached it partly as a journalist and editor but have also drawn on my earlier background as a student of international relations. I acknowledge that not everyone will have the same views on the international system as I do, but I hope that this book will at least set them thinking.

I should like to thank Rik Medlik, without whose initial promptings I would probably never have got round to setting finger to keyboard, for his help and encouragement. I should also like to thank Tony Seaton for voicing – albeit in the unacademic setting of a dinner party – the observation that tourism has given so many people so much pleasure, an observation which aided the writing of Chapter 10. The many contributors to *Tourism Management* and other books and journals on tourism have also stimulated my ideas, while Kathryn Grant and Diane Scarlett at Butterworth-Heinemann have been supportive and patient. Finally, I should like to thank Derek Hall for his valuable comments on earlier drafts and his suggestions for further reading, but above all for his moral support and understanding.

I am grateful to Constable Publishers for permission to quote an extract from *Journey through Britain* by John Hillaby.

Frances Brown

NEWCASTLE-UNDER-LYME
COLLEGE LEARNING
RESOURCES

Abbreviations and acronyms

CER	Closer Economic Relations [agreement]
CRS	computer reservations system
EIA	environmental impact assessment
EU	European Union
FO	Foreign Office
FSU	former Soviet Union
GATS	General Agreement on Trade in Services
GATT	General Agreement on Tariffs and Trade
GNP	gross national product
IATA	International Air Transport Association
IGO	intergovernmental organization
IHA	International Hotel Association
IMF	International Monetary Fund
IO	international organization
IR	international relations
IUOTO	International Union of Official Tourism Organizations
LDCs	less developed countries
MNC	multinational corporation
NAFTA	North American Free Trade Agreement
NGO	non-governmental organization
NTO	National Tourist Office
OPEC	Organization of Petroleum Exporting Countries
R&D	research and development
SMEs	small and medium-sized businesses
TNC	transnational corporation
TOSG	Tour Operators Study Group
UN	United Nations

UNDP	United Nations Development Programme
UNESCO	United Nations Educational Scientific and Cultural Organization
VR	virtual reality
WTO	World Tourism Organization
WTTC	World Travel and Tourism Council
WTTERC	World Travel and Tourism Environment Research Centre

Part One

The Context

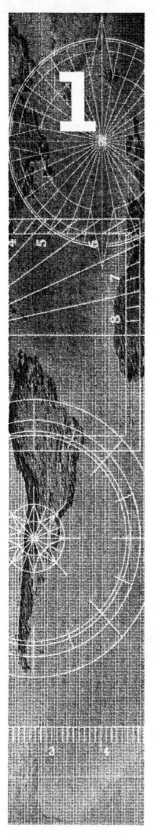

Introduction

In the three-mile walk from Lanyon quoit to the coast you move in and out of hut circles, settlements, burial mounds, Iron Age forts and Celtic stones, but, apart from advertisements for ice-cream and Pepsi Cola, there isn't a noticeboard or signpost in this layer cake of prehistory. The monuments are tucked away in corners of fields; they lie on hilltops, where they are largely defaced or partly obscured by rank vegetation. For this the Ministry of Public Building and Works is largely to blame.

(John Hillaby, *Journey Through Britain*)

These observations by one of the world's great walkers were first published in 1968. What would John Hillaby, who died in 1996, have made of the situation today? Now, in Cornwall and the rest of the UK, the advertisements have been replaced with a forest of brown signposts indicating a historical or natural site to the tourist. No ancient monument, stately home, local museum or waterfall is too obscure, it seems, to merit one, and the situation is much the same in other countries.

Hillaby could no longer complain that such sites are neglected, nor that the public is thereby denied access to them. But as a man who believed in doing things on his own, he might well have been dismayed at the numbers now flocking to some of his favourite areas. In this, too, he would not be alone. For in some, mainly academic, circles tourism has come to be one of the most denigrated activities on Earth, while still being portrayed as a virtual panacea in others, notably industry and government. How can the adoption of such divergent positions have occurred?

A few facts

That the 'tourism industry', made up of activities in the sectors of transport, accommodation, catering, retailing, historical and other attraction management, is one of the world's largest and most significant in terms of turnover, employment and visibility, is well known and does not require a long regurgitation of statistics. Suffice to say that by 1991 international tourism receipts were already making up 1.5 per cent of world gross national product (GNP), a share which had doubled since 1980 (Vellas and Becherel, 1995: 240, table 8.4). In 1996 some 594 million international visitor arrivals were recorded worldwide – a rise of 5.32 per cent over 1995 (WTO, 1997a) and a figure which does not even include the many more domestic vistors who are tourists within their own countries; they spent a total of US$423 million on tourism services, excluding transport (WTO, 1997a). By 1997, according to some perhaps overgenerous estimates (Bar-On, 1997: 409, table 9), there were 262 million people employed in the tourism industry around the world. Even allowing for the difficulties of obtaining accurate data that are comparable across countries, these statistics are impressive.

Equally well known is the fact that the wealth generated by this industry often does not reach the people, destinations and economies hoping to benefit from it, particularly those in developing countries, and that tourism's impact is not confined to economics. Because of the numbers involved, tourism has an effect on the natural and built (especially historic) environments, as well as on local infrastructures. Because tourists are taken to the product, rather than the other way round, their massive presence has an effect on cultural and social behaviour. And because it takes place on a global scale, tourism also has an effect on international relations.

It is no surprise, then, that researchers should wish to study this phenomenon, nor that large numbers of them should have become critical of it. What is more surprising is that few have looked far beyond the tourism industry for the reasons for its alleged iniquities, preferring to personify it as a free agent. Take, for example, this quote from Marie-Françoise Lanfant and

Nelson Graburn, 'Thus culture, society, and identity become mass products when International Tourism enters a country' (Lanfant and Graburn, 1992: 97), a statement which implies that tourism is an independent force acting in a vacuum. Further, researchers do not seem to have compared its impacts with those of other industries and activities, nor have they attempted to suggest economic and non-travel leisure activities that could take its place. In other words, they have tended to see it as a discrete – albeit global – activity to be judged without reference to the sum of economic activities and social trends of which it is a part. Yet tourism cannot be understood in isolation outside this context.

Positions adopted

According to Jafari (1989), research and writing on tourism can be divided into four groups, or 'platforms', which, while arising chronologically, are all still current today. The *advocacy* platform focuses largely on tourism's economic contribution and promotes it as a major means of development without considering any other factors. The *cautionary* approach – which began as a reaction against its predecessor – questions assumptions of economic benefit and highlights negative aspects of the social, cultural and environmental impacts of tourism.

In response to this, the *adaptancy* platform has emphasized the way tourism is changing to adapt to new demands (see Poon, 1993) and highlighted new (non-mass) forms of tourism that are thought to provide its advantages while minimizing its disadvantages. It is also the champion of such concepts as 'alternative tourism', 'ecotourism' and 'sustainable tourism', concepts which have themselves been attacked as elitist and an insufficient, even economically harmful, response by Wheeller (1991, 1993) and Butler (1992) among others. The fourth platform, the *knowledge-based* platform, comprises attempts to produce a scientific body of knowledge on tourism which is theoretically grounded in the social sciences (Dann, 1996) and which will contribute to a holistic study of it while 'simultaneously maintain[ing] bridges with other platforms' (Jafari, 1989: 25), suggesting an interdisciplinary approach, but one that will also look at the whole as well as the parts.

However, even within recent work, which has ranged widely across economics, geography, environmental sciences, psychology, sociology and anthropology, there is still little consideration given to the political aspects of tourism. Nor has much attention been paid to its place in the wider world and thus to the whole of which tourism is part. The few exceptions include Richter (1989) and Hall (1994), while Enloe (1990) has added a feminist slant. There seems to be little awareness that tourism is contingent upon a particular political–economic system or that, rather than being simply an autonomous – and often harmful – actor in its own right, tourism and its impacts are a manifestation of wider political processes, although Urry (1990, 1995) has made a convincing case for seeing it as the manifestation of socio-cultural processes. It is the aim of this book therefore to concentrate on this wider context in order to investigate how the impacts of tourism are conditioned by its place in the global system; how far any of the other activities that make up this system could provide a valid economic alternative or substitute for its more harmful effects; and how far significant change for the better is precluded by that system. The aim is not to provide an exhaustive catalogue of tourism's impacts for good or ill – several writers have already made an admirable job of this – but to reassess these impacts in the light of current economic and political processes.

For there is of course already a large literature on the impacts of tourism, which can leave us in no doubt about its pervasive influence. Sir George Young (1973) was one of the first to highlight tourism's negative aspects at a time when the industry was regarded almost universally as a force for (economic) good. His essentially UK-based analysis has been followed by more wide-ranging works (e.g. Mathieson and Wall, 1982; Archer and Cooper, 1994), most of which concentrate on tourism in developing countries (Shivji, 1973; Bryden, 1973; Turner and Ash, 1975; de Kadt, 1979; Harrison, 1992; Eber, 1992), though some have analysed certain sectors of the tourism industry in the developed world (e.g. Hewison, 1987). Krippendorf (1987) included in his critique consideration of why people feel the need to go on holiday and laid the blame for this on twentieth-century urban living, while Urry (1990, 1995) has identified tourism as an exemplification of the cultural trends of contemporary, 'postmodern' society. A large body of case studies on the subject of impacts has also been published in the major tourism journals (*Annals of Tourism Research, Tourism Management, Journal of Travel Research, Journal of Tourism Studies, Progress in Tourism and Hospitality Research* and *Tourism Recreation Research*).

This rapidly expanding literature has increased our understanding of the workings of tourism and has rightly been influential. But none of the texts cited above has more than partially taken account of the wider political context within which tourism takes place, nor fully attempted to balance all sides within the many grey areas that surround tourism activities. The problem has, in simplified terms, been summed up by a former Fijian finance minister, quoted in Turner and Ash (1975: 166): 'I don't want to see the country of my birth ruined by millions of visitors running over it. But neither do I want to live in a poverty stricken country.' In other words, you can't have benefits without some costs, particularly in view of the vast number of conflicting interests in the world today. Indeed, in many countries, it is debatable whether such a thing as 'the national interest' exists at all. Inevitably, this makes the equitable organization of *any* industry problematic, yet many researchers tend to write as if tourism creates, rather than highlights, divisiveness.

It is the contention, then, that by paying greater attention to the interests at work behind the practice of tourism we will gain a better understanding of why its impacts are as they are. For how else can one explain the fact that, despite the enormous amount of academic material devoted to criticizing tourism and tourists, or pleading for a change in behaviour, it has all but been ignored by the tourism industry itself? (There has long been a non-meeting of minds between practitioners of tourism and those who study it; neither side seems capable of putting itself in the other's shoes.) How can one explain that the policy recommendations on tourism development adopted by UNESCO and the World Bank at a seminar in 1976 (de Kadt, 1979: 339–47) – still one of the soundest and most sensitive such documents – have at best only ever been partially followed by governments and local authorities? Is the tourism industry simply evil or is it rather constrained to act in certain ways that preclude a more equitable distribution of costs and benefits?

The lack of attention paid by tourism researchers to this issue is repeated to an even more startling degree within the political science and international relations disciplines themselves (Linda Richter and Dennis Judd being the honourable exceptions here). A search through a UK university database has revealed not one title linking tourism with international relations out of 15,782 possibilities surveyed. This shortcoming and the possible reasons for it will be discussed in Chapter 2, and the ways in which tourism can be theorized as a factor in international relations presented. In particular, tourism's role (or not) in the spread of globalization will be analysed.

Chapter 3 will build on this by examining concrete examples of the effects of external events and systemic trends (e.g. war, terrorism, currency fluctuations, political change) on tourism. It will consider how the tourism industry itself affects destinations and shapes the political process. Can tourism ever be a force for peace?

In Chapter 4 we will cover tourism's place in the international institutional framework, by examining the role and effectiveness of organizations such as the World Tourism Organization (WTO) and the World Travel and Tourism Council (WTTC), and suggesting that these too reflect broader politico-economic trends. How far – given its fragmented nature – the industry actually is 'institionalized' will be considered, with attention focused on the General Agreement on Trade in Services (GATS) and other supranational regulations, such as that produced by the European Union (EU). Here it will be argued that tourism is being driven by the worldwide trend towards economic integration.

The four chapters in Part Two will be concerned with the specific impacts of tourism – environmental, economic, social and cultural – and with the way in which these are conditioned by the international system. Thus, tourism's environmental impacts will be compared with those of other economic sectors and the reasons for the differences in their scope and treatment between the developed and developing world analysed. Its suitability as a generator of jobs and revenue will be balanced against that of other industries, with particular reference to the illegal drugs trade, in order to investigate whether viable alternatives exist within the global system as it is currently organized.

The ways in which tourism affects both visited and visiting societies will be addressed in Chapter 7 and an attempt made to restore the balance in the incomers v. locals debate: do the former always destroy the societies they came to experience, do they help preserve them or do they act as a catalyst for beneficial change? Crucial to this question is the concept of authenticity, which is also germane to Chapter 8 on tourism and cultural heritage. This will highlight the diversity of interests involved and how these have shaped various outcomes. These chapters will also look at the evolution of Western attitudes to nature and to the past, themselves influenced by the present state of the global political economy. Certainly they have affected types of tourism development but they have also coloured many researchers' attitudes to what is right and wrong in tourism.

The final part of the book will take some tentative steps towards identifying whether anything can be done if tourism continues on its upward trajectory. Chapter 9 will evaluate the validity of the arguments put forward by writers such as Young, Krippendorf, Turner and Ash, and de Kadt, and discuss the practicability and desirability of their prescriptions. The scope for 'alternative tourism' to provide an answer to the problems created by tourism will also be examined.

This will entail consideration of how far proposed solutions to the problems of tourism take account of the prevailing organization of the global system and of people's motivation to travel, which will lead us to Chapter 10's discussion of why people become tourists. This will examine the positive effects of tourism on tourists and look at the way travel came to symbolize freedom for Eastern Europeans post-1989. It will contest the applicability of the thesis that travel is only a means of escape in favour of viewing it as a human imperative and speculate – that being the case – on whether anything can change this.

A conclusion will attempt to draw together the conflicting elements that make up the impacts of tourism and discuss whether the current global system makes its adverse effects inevitable, or precludes radical change. Is there a way of reconciling the divergent interests that now operate at all levels of the system? The final chapter will look at the future, with an appraisal of the direction tourism may take, given the above, and of developments such as virtual reality. It will aso consider Urry's (1995: 147–50) suggestion that its status as the ultimate postmodern phenomenon, its very ubiquity, will lead to the end of tourism.

A brief history – *plus ça change?*

The growing popularity of 'postmodern' analyses of tourism have fostered the belief that tourism is a purely twentieth-century phenomenon – which of course it is not. While its huge scale and accessibility to most (though still not all) levels of Western societies are undeniably recent, its essential character-istics, and its dependence on certain political and technological conditions, seem unchanged. (For a comprehensive treatment of the history of tourism in the West, see Towner, 1996.)

Just as today, early tourism was facilitated by external, often publicly funded developments. Roman road construction encouraged travel from the city to country villas and resorts around the Bay of Naples, while General Wade's eighteenth-century military roads aided the spread of tourism in Scotland (Seaton, 1996b). It was also stimulated by improved methods of transport (e.g. the invention of the stagecoach, which considerably reduced travelling time) and by a stable political environment such as existed for two centuries of the Roman empire. And in the same way that the prospect of increasing visitor numbers has spurred modern governments to build hotels, runways, even whole new airports, so early tourism provided an impetus to the building of hotels along the banks of the Nile during Roman times, to the establishment of accommodation, eating places and shops along Europe's pilgrimage routes in the Middle Ages and to the improvement of roads in eighteenth-century Britain through turnpiking (the first turnpike act was passed in Kent in 1709 specifically in order to improve access to Tunbridge Wells spa).

Tourism in the past was as much concerned with pleasure and a change of environment, or escape from unpleasant weather, as it is today, witness the

Roman fascination with Egypt mentioned above, the growth of country homes around the Bosphorous during the Ottoman empire and the Chinese penchant for building 'pleasure houses' with water gardens and shady groves from the eleventh century onwards (Towner, 1995: 341). It was also strongly influenced by fashion and a desire for prestige, with no less a figure than the emperor Hadrian having notice of his visit to the Colossi of Memnon scratched on to one of the statues for posterity (Balmer, 1996) and the English aristocracy following the Prince Regent to Brighton as faithfully as latter-day 'wannabes' followed Brigitte Bardot to St Tropez.

Finally, there is little indication that early tourists and tour guides were any better behaved or more honest than are some sections of those involved in tourism today. The Campanian resort of Baiae, which was frequented by wealthy Romans, became a byword for ostentatious display and unseemly behaviour. Hadrian was not the only ancient person to deface monuments – his wife's companion's poems join over 100 other scratchings; think of the wealth of graffiti, much of it lewd, at Pompeii. And the nun Egeria, who made a pilgrimage to the Holy Land in the fourth century AD, was surely being duped when she mentions, in her *Peregrinatio ad loca sancta*, being shown the exact spot where God spoke to Moses from the burning bush.

So is there anything else besides numbers and its spread through the social classes that differentiates tourism today from that of earlier times? Is it so specifically postmodern, or would its features be roughly similar in any system in which power is not distributed equally? Again, we can only look at the context within which it is carried out – basically that of late capitalist society – to find out. That is what this book hopes to do.

2

Tourism's place within international relations

> Tourism is not just a matter of national growth, but must be conceptualized as part of international relations.
>
> (Lanfant and Graburn, 1992: 94)

If the literature on tourism emanating from departments of tourism studies, and others like economics, geography and sociology that offer courses on tourism, has been growing exponentially, consideration of the phenomenon within the fields of political science and international relations (IR) has been sadly lacking. Yet, as Hall (1994: 59) has rightly noted: 'By its increasingly international nature, tourism is inseparable from the field of international relations'.

For, while numbers of domestic tourists in the industrialized countries still greatly exceed those who travel abroad, tourism between countries has grown more than twentyfold since 1950 (WTO, 1997a). It would be extraordinary if such movement was not shaped by the economic and political relations between different states, and equally extraordinary if it did not affect the course of those relations. Tourism involves large quantities of currency exchanges, whose value may be enhanced or all but wiped out by stock market fluctuations or changes in government economic policy. Much of the industry, particularly tour operation and air transport, is controlled by multinational corporations – who have belatedly been acknowledged as actors within IR – operating across national boundaries. Political and economic upheavals in one part of the world may affect travel to and from other parts, altering tourism flows and producing a knock-on economic effect. Governments can impose tourism 'sanctions' that are every bit as effective as commodity embargoes. Some countries have used tourism to help solve balance of trade surpluses, to project a particular image or to promote their own ideology. The very establishment and operation of a tourism industry can be viewed (depending on one's perspective and political leanings) either as a means to development, modernization and 'progress' or as an example of structural dependency and neocolonial exploitation.

These are just a few examples of the many ways in which tourism is bound up with international affairs. The relationship between the two will be explored in further detail below before we turn to an examination of tourism's role in the trend towards globalization. But we will start with a discussion of the reasons for tourism's absence from the field of IR.

The neglect of tourism in international relations

The lack of attention paid to tourism by political scientists (of whom IR researchers may be considered a subset) was noted as early as 1975 by Mathews and has been well documented by Richter (1983). Her article enumerates the characteristics of tourism, which would repay study for their political relevance, and discusses the subfields of politics in which tourism plays a role. They include policy studies, comparative politics, public administration, political thought and IR itself; in a response to a commentary on her article (Richter, 1984) she suggests that incidents like the Soviet shooting down of a Korean Airlines jet in 1983 could mean that tourism first reaches the political study agenda through IR. Yet, despite her compelling argument, the situation has scarcely improved in the last fifteen years. The dearth of books on tourism and international relations has already been mentioned and an examination of the contents of 1990s issues of the main IR journals (*Foreign Affairs, International Affairs* and *World Politics*) yields equal disappointment. Not even the *New Left Review*, traditionally a more radical and wide-ranging journal, which has frequently covered the environment, feminism and postmodernism, for instance, has tackled the subject. In recent years it has published two articles on ecofeminism, but none on ecotourism. What can be the reasons for this?

First and foremost, and despite the broadening of scope evident in journals like the *New Left Review*, IR theory remains obsessed with 'high politics' – i.e. the doings of governments – with the notion of the state as actor and with issues of security and competition. Despite extensive media coverage and work in some academic departments on the rise of transnational corporations – many with far more economic and political influence than some small states – and on the significance of globalization, of non-governmental organizations (NGOs) and environmental or women's movements, these trends have received scant coverage in IR publications. Even those less mainstream journals (e.g. *Third World Quarterly, New Political Economy*) which aim to give greater emphasis to non-state politics, or to provide a new approach to what they see as a new world order, have not seen fit to consider tourism as part of that world order.

The end of the Cold War, which admittedly changed a rather stable, if potentially lethal, bipolar situation into a much more uncertain and hence unstable one, has done nothing to dampen study of national security. And while many authors now see economic security as of growing significance following the decline in the threat of global (as opposed to regional) conflict, few have attempted to analyse how tourism – one of the most important economic activities worldwide – fits into this.

Second, for all its economic weight, tourism still is not taken seriously in many academic circles. For surely the 'business of fun' is too trivial for serious study? The labels of a 'candyfloss industry' creating 'Mickey Mouse jobs' seem to have stuck; because some jobs in the industry are still seasonal and low paid, tourism is not deemed worthy of attention. Yet these very facts could have provoked interest in why this is so and they confirm Enloe's (1990: 40) remark: 'That tourism is not discussed as seriously by conventional political commentators as oil or weaponry may tell us more about the ideological construction of "seriousness" than about the politics of tourism'. Instead, however, tourism politics have been studied as a dimension of larger concerns such as development: 'While other industries – the politics of oil or energy, for example – have become popular *foci* of political research, world tourism has not' (Mathews, 1975: 197).

Third, as Kosters (1984) has identified, tourism is a fragmented industry. Indeed, some analysts (e.g. Leiper, 1979, 1990) would reject altogether the notion that tourism is an industry. Whatever the merits of this argument, it is true that tourism is made up of large numbers of small and individually owned businesses alongside the mega-corporations. It is also divided into specialized areas of business such as transport, marketing and accommodation which tend to be regarded and studied as discrete entities.

Atomization and separation

This leads us to a further possible cause of neglect – the academic division of labour. What is meant by this is the way separate departments (geography, sociology) have been set up to study different aspects of our social reality and, in particular, the way in which politics and economics are kept apart. The latter applies not only academically, but also institutionally, so that institutions like the World Bank and the International Monetary Fund (IMF) profess to be concerned only with solving the world's economic problems, while political problems are left to the United Nations (UN) General Assembly or to regional organizations such as the Conference on Security and Cooperation in Europe. The early 1980s row over the 'politicization' of the United Nations Educational Scientific and Cultural Organization (UNESCO) illustrates the desire to see politics and economics as different, even irreconcilable, entities. When it tried to promote a 'new international information order' to mirror the 'new international economic order' demanded by developing countries, the USA and the UK, who were major funders of UNESCO, both withdrew from the organization; the former has still not rejoined it.

The separation of politics and economics in turn shapes the way IR has been looked at and the kind of issues that have been studied – which in its turn may even shape IR activity itself (McLean, 1981), by implying that action outside the 'given' framework is impossible. Tourism, for example, is still largely seen as an economic rather than a political phenomenon. This bias has been acknowledged by Hall, who notes (1994: 110–11) that: 'The selection of a particular theory or approach to development by the researcher or policy analyst will set the boundaries within which research is conducted, conclusions are reached and recommendations made.' He goes on to suggest that tourism studies may not be able to 'transcend the capitalistic nature of most tourism consumption and production' because this also affects the way researchers are funded (Hall, 1994: 111).

However, if the notion that politics and economics are separate is rejected, a case can be made for considering the international system in general and tourism in particular as a synthesis, or fusion, of the various parts, including economics and politics, which go to make them up. In the same way that different plants flourish or wither depending on the way sunshine, water and soil all combine to produce them, the world we live in can be seen as the result of a process to which both economics and politics contribute. By this reckoning, when we move to explain either politics or economics, each is necessary to the other (Wood, 1981).

Such a method of study is, however, rarely attempted in IR, which limits itself either to the atomistic approach of breaking a subject down into discrete units, or the systemic approach of viewing the international system as subject to macrolaws that are not affected by the behaviour of individual units but do affect the way these units are arranged in the system. The first method is basically reductionist, while the second is mechanistic and appears to negate the idea of free will. Both take current social reality as given and therefore serve to reinforce that reality and discourage other ways of conceiving it. What may be more helpful is a holistic approach which is able to consider the international system both as a number of parts with differing influences and as a whole that is greater than the sum of these parts and in turn influences them.

In the case of tourism, such an approach would allow it to be considered in multifarious ways: as the product of specific (economic, social, etc.) activities, as a force creating a variety of localized impacts and an element affecting wider world economic and political processes, and as one of the many phenomena whose practice is conditioned by international capitalism. A similar view has been expressed by Lanfant (1980) in her assertion that the grounding of tourism study in the 'reality' of supply and demand economics allows it to ignore social and cultural issues. She sees tourism as created by a network of agents. Piecemeal investigation of these agents would be reductionist she argues, but she also rejects taking a mechanistic view of the social system. Strangely, she does not name politics as one of the agents behind the creation of tourism. Small wonder then that even those who do support a holistic approach to the study of IR have not yet come to consider tourism as a microcosm of the economic, social and political processes of which today's social reality is the result.

But if we do try and conceive of it in this way, we may come nearer to understanding the context in which tourism takes place and thus whether, within such a context, there is any alternative to the way it occurs. Let us now look at the ways in which tourism is part of IR by attempting to identify how it is affected by economic and political processes.

Tourism, politics and economics

Several examples of tourism's relationship to international relations have been summarized previously in this chapter. A more comprehensive list of IR concerns and how they can influence tourist activities, together with a list of the ways in which tourism itself may influence international relations is presented in Table 2.1.

As we can see, the relationship is wide-ranging. Specific examples will be discussed in Chapter 3 but, for now, the important thing to note is how Table 2.1 shows that fusion of economic and political phenomena shape tourism, which itself has indissoluble political and economic impacts. For example, two countries may encourage their tourism industries in order to increase their income, but if one permits only organized tours to what it considers are its showcase farms, factories and similar locations in order to display the rightness of its political system, while the other targets high-spending niche tourists in order to promote the image of a high-class destination, their industries will look very different. To take another example, terrorists may target tourists in order to scare them from visiting a given country – thereby harming its economy – in order to make a political point; the tourists may switch (or be switched by a tour operator) to another country, thereby increasing the latter's export earnings and enriching certain sections of the population who start to command more political power. Finally, a tour operator's decision to sell holidays in one country over another may cause economic repercussions in the other country that lead to pressure for a change of government (though not necessarily to a pro-tourism one).

A role in globalization?

Tourism can now clearly be seen as a facet of the international political economy, producing demonstrable effects on it. But does that make its role a determining one? To close the chapter we shall examine tourism's part within what is now perceived as one of the major trends of international relations activity – globalization.

Characteristics of globalization

There is no universally accepted definition of globalization but it is generally understood to encompass the following trends:

- the worldwide spread of a neoliberal capitalist system
- the growth of transnational companies (TNCs), able to operate free of national restrictions
- an increase in the speed and flow of capital in money form
- the use of computerized and satellite relayed technology which inhibits national regulation of information flows

Table 2.1   Ways in which international relations and tourism influence each other

IR concerns	Tourism-related effects
War/conflict	Discourages visitors to within a wide radius; knock-on economic impact; tourism infrastructure damaged
Economic competition	Tourism chosen as 'easy' to implement
Currency movements/ devaluations/inflation	Tour operators and tourists switch to cheaper countries
Global integration	Tourism draws 'traditional' or isolationist societies into global mainstream
Growth/development/ restructuring	Tourism supplants agriculture in LDCs; replaces manufacturing in DCs
Neocolonialism, core–periphery relationships	Tourism as agent of perpetuation of colonially imposed structural dependency
Secessionist/independence/ radical change movements	Target tourists to hurt government financially or draw attention to cause
Promotion of ideology/way of life	Tourism as image enhancer, notably via mega-events
Discouragement of others' ideology or policies	Travel embargoes; extra-territorial legislation
International co-operation	Regional marketing strategies
Deregulation	Higher/lower fares; better/worse service; travel safety issues
Sovereignty	Country may facilitate tourism to disputed territory to strengthen its claim (Hall, 1994: 87)
Flows of people across borders	Possible regional integration; may foreshadow or predict aid flows (Young, in Richter, 1983: 324)
Currency flows across borders	International balance of trade affected
Foreign/outside investment in destinations	New political power arrangements; rise of new interests
Demonstration effect	Social changes which may be welcomed or not by governments
Imposition or removal of visa requirements	Barometer of countries' relations and alliances
High visibility of tourists	Potential target for disgruntled groups

17

- growing interdependence among states, leading to a blurring of boundaries as economic or political events in one country have an effect way beyond its borders
- greater knowledge of the world and a perception that it has 'shrunk' thanks to television, the internet and high-speed transportation links
- reflexivity, i.e. the possibility of evaluating and monitoring one's own culture and society, and their place in the world, by comparison with those of others, which may lead to cultural homogenization, as implied by the above, but may also lead to efforts to retain national or local control and to emphasize cultural differences (Sharpley, 1994: 237–9; Waters, 1995: 3–4; Urry, 1995; Marshall, 1996).

Implicit within this is the notion (so loftily ignored by most writers on IR) of the demise of the nation-state and the rise of actors such as TNCs, NGOs and interest groups (women, ethnic minorities, Islamists, Greens) united across geographical and political divides.

We should perhaps note here that the concept of globalization remains a contested one and that several authors believe reports of the death of the nation-state have been greatly exaggerated (see for example Jones, 1995; Hirst and Thompson, 1996; Marshall, 1996). There are many situations (e.g. national security) where states still yield far greater power than other actors and the debate on the balance of power between state and non-state actors will run and run. But the fact that the latter exist and that observable changes have taken place in the global political economy cannot be denied.

Tourism and globalization: driver or driven?

Tourism exemplifies many aspects of globalization. The spread of tourism to the farthest reaches of the planet, and people's willingness to travel to places their parents had never even heard of (if we are to believe some reports, many tourists have not heard of them either) demonstrate the extent to which tourists themselves conceptualize the world as a single place (Waters, 1995: 155). Aspects of the industry are becoming dominated by large multinational corporations (MNCs) which, thanks to vertical and horizontal integration, own or control businesses involved in all stages of the tourism process – tour operators, airlines, hotels – and operate transnationally. This gives them an ability to dictate to tourists, small businesses and even certain destinations (Sharpley, 1994: 241). The presence and visibility of tourists in countries other than their own has been linked to cultural homogenization, to the spread of a dominant (mainly US) culture and, through their penchant for shopping, to the commodification of culture.

There is no doubt, then, that tourism can be viewed as a globalizing process, but can it be said to have helped instigate that process, or is it constructed in response to it?

Certainly, a previously unvisited country with a subsistence agriculture economy that decided to develop a tourism industry would inevitably find itself drawn into the international system – through the need to export its product – but this would be the case with the development of any other service or manufacturing industry. Tourism is a *means* of bringing states into the international economy but it is the structure of the economy itself which dictates that any export-orientated strategy will involve incorporation into the world system. Tourism has indeed grown thanks to large firms' economies of scale enabling prices to be kept low, but it would never have spread without the advances in transport and technology that make travel so much easier and faster, without the increase in leisure time brought about by changes in working practices, nor indeed without the period of global peace that has followed the Second World War. Tourism cannot exist without suitable political and economic conditions and cannot create these on its own.

It is technological advances, particularly in communications, that are also responsible for people's growing conception of the world as a single place. (One of its most powerful representations is the image of the Earth taken from space.) Indeed, where states have reacted to the spread of interdependence by making efforts to reassert their differences – the countries of the EU, especially France, are good examples – tourism has the potential to show people that the world is not as undifferentiated as they thought. And while tourism can contribute to cultural homogenization through the demonstration effect, whereby hosts may want to copy their visitors' dress and behaviour, and through the erection of characterless corporate hotels and outlets selling 'international (i.e. bland) cuisine' it is by no means the only culprit. Again, the spread of communications, especially films and television, and the worldwide export of standardized manufactures, have had a far bigger hand in this.

But what of the transnational power of companies like Thomas Cook, American Express or Thomson? Vertical integration has certainly given them more power over the stages of the holiday production process, but in this they are merely mirroring trends within retail and manufacturing, trends, moreover, which have always been present in capitalism. More pertinently, they all have an identifiable national base. Just as doubt has been sown over the validity of the globalization thesis, so there is scepticism about how far internationally operating firms really are transnational (controlled by nationals of a variety of countries) as opposed to multinational ('nationally embedded' [Hirst and

Thompson, 1996] but active in many countries). Marshall (1996: 879) reports that an examination of the ownership of stock illustrates that so-called TNCs are usually owned and controlled by capitalists from a single core state. While a sizeable proportion of sales and a lesser precentage of production may take place abroad, executive boards, management styles and research and development (R&D) can all be traced to the core state. Again, tourism companies follow this pattern, except for a higher concentration of 'production facilities' (i.e. destinations) abroad. This is not to deny their power over some foreign economies but rather to illustrate their similarity to other sectors. They have not been blazing a trail.

In fact, if true globalization is to take place, future patterns will feature the downscaling of companies so that core large firms are increasingly unable to dominate the producers marketing globally (Waters, 1995: 92). Evidence for this is seen in new co-operative arrangements being put in place, such as joint ventures, alliances (common in the airline industry), marketing agreements, off-shore component production and cross-cutting equity ownership, and in the fact that some less developed countries (LDCs) (notably the East Asian 'tigers') have become rivals to, rather than producers for, the industrialized countries (Gilpin, 1987: 256). Emmott (in Waters, 1995: 80) has even argued that, in a truly globalized economy, MNCs would give way to local producers marketing globally. The tourism giants may be about to turn into dinosaurs! More probably, they will adapt; conceivably, given the earlier cited reservations about globalization, a fully globalized economy will not come to pass. Whatever the case, the above discussion should have illustrated that, while tourism has certainly aided the spread of globalization, it has done this more by reflecting the characteristics of the external system of which it is a part, rather than by itself creating globalizing processes. We will examine its place in the world economy more closely in Chapter 6.

3

Tourism and external events — a two-way influence

As Urry (1990: 64) has noted: 'It is important to appreciate that the growth of tourism in developing countries ... does not simply derive from processes internal to those societies. Such a development possibility results from a number of external conditions.' One might add that it is not simply developing countries, but all countries, that are affected by external conditions and that it is not just the establishment of tourism but its day-to-day practice that is affected by them.

Since we have discussed some of the external conditions that mediate the relationship between tourism and international relations in the previous chapter, we shall now turn to specific examples of their impact, and of the way in which tourism itself can influence events.

For a start, tourism as we know it today would not exist without the technological advances made during and after the two world wars. These included the mass production of automobiles, which led to a boom in domestic travel in Europe and the USA, the invention of the jet engine and development of wide-bodied aircraft, the spread of television, whose pictures opened people's eyes to the rest of the world, and progress in computing and miniaturization, leading to computerized reservation services, initially for air transport, but now for almost everything.

War and terrorism

It is ironic that advances in aircraft design were stimulated by both world wars, since war and conflict, which probably have the most disruptive effect on 'normal' everyday activities, are a major deterrent to tourism. While it might seem obvious that few tourists would want to visit countries with an ongoing history of conflict, such as Chad, Afghanistan, Algeria, Cambodia, or Lebanon, which had a vibrant tourism industry before civil war broke out in 1975, more striking is the way the outbreak of war can cause people to avoid unaffected countries in the same region in their droves. A most recent example of this was Cyprus during the Persian Gulf war of early 1991, where both the north and south of the island saw arrivals that year plummet after a lengthy period of growth. Even more bizarre was the marked reluctance of Americans to fly to Europe during this period and following the US bombing of Libya in 1986. This may be partly the result of poor geography teaching and the USA's traditionally parochial view of 'abroad', but it does illustrate the far-reaching effects that conflict can have. Indeed, destination countries were not the only parties affected: ten UK tour operators collapsed in the first three months of 1991 thanks to the combined impact of recession and the Gulf war (Middleton, 1991: 185).

Nevertheless, the numbers visiting both Europe in general and Cyprus in particular did bounce back rapidly in 1992, suggesting that, if war is one of the quickest turn-offs, the unambiguous expectation of peace is an equally powerful draw (see below). Northern Ireland is an instructive case here. Although technically an arena for terrorist acts, the province has been shunned by many as a war zone and tourism remained at a low level throughout the time of the euphemistically named 'troubles'. But, following the IRA ceasefire in August 1994 and the subsequent Loyalist cessation of military operations, tourism activity began to grow. Total visitor numbers to the province increased by some 17 per cent to a record 1.5 million in 1995 and average hotel room occupancy rates rose by 11 percentage points on 1994 to 62 per cent (O'Neill and Fitz, 1996). Moreover, large hotel companies such as Hilton and Holiday Inn, along with domestic entrepreneurs, put forward hotel proposals that would amount to £200 million worth of investment. The Sea Cat catamaran service between Belfast and Stranraer was relaunched and a major supermarket chain, Sainsbury's, announced plans for seven new stores. Then came the ending of the ceasefire in February 1996 – and an equally sudden cessation of enquiries to the Northern Ireland Tourist Board. A £240 million European investment package was also put on hold (O'Neill and Fitz, 1996: 162). At the time of writing a full-scale Peace Agreement is in place but the optimism that accompanied the first ceasefire is less marked. It will be interesting to see how far tourists and investors are now prepared to give the 'peace process' in Northern Ireland a second chance.

Northern Ireland has yet to 'take off' as a tourist region but terrorism can also have a dramatic effect on visitor numbers in more established destinations. Like war, it can adversely affect third countries. The reason for many Americans' reluctance to cross the Atlantic during the Gulf war was fear of being blown up by a terrorist bomb, something that has consistently kept visitor numbers to the Middle East lower than they could be relative to the attractions of the region. Organized tourism virtually disappeared from Sri Lanka at the height of the Tamil Tiger insurgency and it was possible to bargain a room in a five-star hotel down to $40, with clearly disastrous consequences for the economy. Yet this was a place where tourists might only incidentally become caught up in an attack.

In Peru, visitor numbers have still not recovered from the dive started in the mid-1980s when the Sendero Luminoso group announced it would target tourists, and this despite the fact that their leader, Abimael Guzman, was captured in 1995. A similar situation exists in Kashmir, where all that is known of the fate of six backpackers kidnapped in 1995 is that at least one of them is dead. In Egypt, where since 1992 tourists, among others, have found themselves targets of assaults by Muslim groups, almost 100 tourists have died. Visitor numbers dropped from a high of 3.2 million in 1992 to 2.5 million in 1993 and 2.6 million in 1994, while receipts almost halved between 1992 and 1994 (WTO, 1997a). Numbers were recovering well by 1995 but, after the attack on a bus outside the Cairo Museum and the slaughter of a tourist group in Luxor in 1997, the country was almost deserted by tourists (*The Times*, 31 December 1997). Tour operators were reduced to offering heavily discounted deals (under £250 for a week's trip) in an effort to offload their 'stock' (*Independent*, 19 September 1997). Airtours cited loss of business to Egypt as a cause of higher than average first quarter losses in 1997/8 (*Independent*, 19 February 1998).

As these figures show, tourists are not the only parties to be harmed by terrorism – local elites, foreign tour operators and the whole national economy can be acutely affected – and it is for this reason that tourists are so useful to terrorists. Richter and Waugh (1991) have argued that there is a logical connection between tourism and terrorism: concentrations of tourists provide cover, especially for international terrorists; their vulnerability away from home makes them easy targets and their transport facilities provide ready-made channels for weapons distribution and escape. Tourists can also be characterized as representatives of their government and therefore provide a means of punishing foreign governments for perceived hostile acts, as with the bombing of a Pan Am flight over Lockerbie in Scotland.

Nevertheless, hurting tourists is not usually the chief object of their attackers. Because of their economic importance, and the fact that the presence of wealthy foreign tourists may be the most obvious manifestation that in some countries economic development has taken no account of the needs of the majority of the local population, they are the target of choice for groups dissatisfied with the *status quo*. Egypt is the example again here: it has been argued that, while Islam is not hostile to tourism *per se*, most Egyptians' experience of tourism is of luxury ghettos providing zero benefits for the local population (Aziz, 1995). Parfitt (1997) points out that unemployment is one of the central factors behind Egypt's problems with terrorism and it follows that disrupting an industry which is perceived to ignore the needs of the poor and unemployed could be considered a legitimate way of getting a government to change its policies. Attacking foreign visitors and businesses is also less likely to alienate the local population. However, there is evidence in Egypt that the success of the 1997 attacks in scaring away tourists backfired: ordinary people as well as foreign firms have lost their tourism-related livelihoods and became thoroughly opposed to the terrorists (*The Times*, 31 December 1997).

Tourists are also highly visible and, where they are from a foreign country, attacking them will almost guarantee international media coverage and draw attention to political causes. The West has been notoriously indifferent to Indonesia's illegal occupation of East Timor and its human rights abuses both there and in Irian Jaya, but the kidnapping of a group of Western scientists by indigenous groups in 1996 at least brought the issue on to the international agenda. Where governments control the news media, targeting foreign tourists may be the only hope that word of a cause gets out (Richter and Waugh, 1991: 323).

Political change

War and terrorism are both (last ditch?) attempts at effecting political change. However, such change can also come about peacefully but still have an impact on tourism. The fall of the Berlin Wall in 1989 completely changed the tourism map of Central and Eastern Europe. The end of Communism in these countries saw an upsurge in visits from the West, especially to Czechoslovakia, Hungary and Poland and a smaller, but equally significant movement of Central and Eastern Europeans westwards. The intra-(ex) Soviet bloc flows which had characterized tourism in the Communist era rapidly declined, but governments began to take tourism more seriously as an employment- and income-generating response to the rising unemployment and fiscal problems created by the transition to a market economy.

Hong Kong is another place that has recently experienced political change in the other direction – from quasi-democratic to Communist rule. The number of mainland Chinese visitors to the former colony has been increasing since China relaxed travel restrictions in the 1980s and it can be expected to grow further now that the latter has incorporated the former. Conversely, the important Taiwanese market, which has been obliged by its government to use a third country (most commonly Hong Kong) as a transit point for visits to the mainland, could decline. If tensions increase, Taiwan could extend its ban on direct visits to the mainland to Hong Kong; if they are eased, direct air links between Taipei and major Chinese cities may ensue, obviating the need to visit Hong Kong (Hobson, 1995: 17). The change in status has also had tourism-related repercussions beyond the immediate region and other tourists are wary of what the handover might mean for them: between July and October 1997 visits by Japanese tourists were down 50 per cent on the previous year (*Today* programme, BBC Radio 4, 22 October 1997). Overall figures for July 1997 show that 480,000 people visited Hong Kong during the handover month, compared with 658,239 for July 1996 – a slump of 32.5 per cent (*Scotland on Sunday*, 30 November 1997). By November of that year, in a rerun of the Egyptian situation, airlines desperate for business were offering return flights from the UK for under £200 and three-night trips for under £300 (*Scotland on Sunday*, 30 November 1997).

Economic influences

The loss of visitors through conflict or political change clearly creates economic winners and losers as tourists switch from affected areas to those perceived as safer or more stable. But economic fluctuations themselves cause changes in behaviour. The strength of the UK pound throughout the summer of 1997 persuaded many people to take a holiday in what had become relatively cheap destinations like France and Spain, rather than staying at home, while deterring others who might have been planning to visit the UK. The consequences for France and Spain were an increase in foreign currency and probably in domestic receipts, too, as some people would have found it too expensive to travel abroad. The UK, on the other hand, found that its tourism deficit had grown. More dramatically, the turmoil on the Asian stock markets in 1997, which caused currencies in the region to plummet in value, turned countries such as Thailand and Malaysia into dream destinations for bargain-hunting tourists, while wiping out profits for local businesses. Such turmoil also exacerbated Hong Kong's problems. In economic terms the effects have been as severe for these countries as any that might have been produced by a terrorist attack.

Tourists as a political and economic tool

The above examples describe events not always under the control of governments; however, there are several situations where governments, who are not directly involved in the tourism industry, deliberately use tourism to further their ends, thereby influencing where and how it takes place. The Japanese government, for example, has used tourism as a way of redressing its huge trade surplus with the USA, actively promoting overseas travel among its citizens through the 'Ten Million Programme' started in 1987 (Polunin, 1989: 5) and easily reaching its target (of having 10 million of its citizens travelling abroad) by 1990. The country now has the highest balance of tourism deficit in the world (Hall, 1994: 73). A similar policy has been followed by Taiwan.

More commonly, governments prevent their people travelling either by imposing outright bans (as formerly in Taiwan and the two Koreas), tight restrictions on which countries could be visited (as in the former Soviet bloc), the use of exit visas, issued at the discretion of the government (the former Soviet bloc again), or by introducing prohibitive travel taxes or limits on domestic currency exports (as in Thailand). A further possibility is prevention of travel to a specific country for political ends. In July 1994 a bloodless coup took place in The Gambia, which had become a popular winter resort for British and Scandinavian holidaymakers, the former representing 60 per cent of all international arrivals to the country in 1993/4 (Sharpley, Sharpley and Adams, 1996). In November 1994 the UK Foreign Office (FO) issued travel advice stating that 'those without compelling reasons to travel should consider postponing their visits'. Almost immediately all UK tour operators but one ceased operations to The Gambia; Scandinavian operators swiftly followed suit. This action resulted in the loss of 1,000 jobs and the closure of at least eight hotels, and affected employment in horticulture, agriculture and brewing. Government income from sales and airport taxes and import duties was also lost (Sharpley, Sharpley and Adams, 1996: 3). Yet there was little evidence to suggest that tourists were at risk from the coup – in any case the FO advice at that time on travel to Egypt, where tourists *had been* at risk of attack, warned only that security could not be guaranteed and stopped short of advising against travel.

Why the FO felt it necessary to impose what amounted to a trade embargo on The Gambia is unclear. It may have feared a loss of influence in the region with a new government installed, or that supporting the latter would undermine US aid policy, which prohibits the provision of aid to countries under military rule (Sharpley, Sharpley and Adams, 1996: 4). What is abundantly clear, however, is the devasting consequences that can follow from the use of tourists as a political weapon.

Interestingly though, the ploy may have backfired in the case of the long-standing US travel ban to Cuba. International tourism in that country has registered major growth since its reintroduction in the 1970s, with Canada providing the highest proportion of visitors, particularly in the winter months. Notwithstanding the ban, a wide range of European countries also contributes large numbers of tourists (Hinch, 1990; Hall, 1992). Between 1989 and 1993 tourist arrivals increased by 73 per cent, while receipts grew by over 350 per cent (Seaton, 1997: 314). Moreover, significant investment in Cuba's industry is now taking place, in the form of joint ventures with Canadian, Dutch, Spanish, Jamaican and British companies (Avella and Mills, 1996: 57). Several US officials privately believe that their tourism industry and investors are losing a golden opportunity for business on their doorstep and fear that, if the travel ban is finally lifted (it was temporarily removed by President Carter in 1977) it will be too late for them to make up ground.

Tourism as image creation

Cuba is also interesting because of the way it has in the past used tourism not only economically to reduce dependence on sugar cane, but also to promote its socialist system. A similar rationale was among the reasons prompting Eastern bloc governments to open their borders to Western tourists in the 1970s, when it was thought that exposure to Communism would convince others of the system's superiority. In other words tourism was seen as a means of promoting a positive image, a fact that was not lost on the Franco and Salazar dictatorships – at the opposite end of the political spectrum – when decisions to develop tourism in Spain and Portugal were made. Elliott (1997: 57) notes that the city government of West Berlin used that city as a tool in the propaganda war between Communist East Germany, the West German government and the whole of the 'free world', but East Berlin, too, symbolized by the massive television tower in Alexanderplatz, was used as a showcase for Communist achievement, its amenities far exceeding those of other cities in East Germany.

Image creation lends itself to the promotion of only those areas of society a government wants outsiders to see, which means that tourism can be the unwitting dupe of repressive regimes or of those presiding over great inequality. However, while individual tourists may visit Turkey's beaches and architecture, or Burma's temples and smiling people in ignorance of the disgraceful human rights abuses common in both countries, the proliferation of media which now bypass government control means that embarassing information can circulate more freely. Burma's efforts to create a tourism boom in 1996 failed largely because of public awareness of its appalling regime. Image creation is more likely to be successful when the areas emphasized bear more relation to the reality experienced by at least a sizeable proportion of society.

One of the more interesting recent examples of governments using tourism for political ends is provided by the Croatian city of Dubrovnik. During the war over the break-up of Yugoslavia, Serbs and Montenegrins deliberately shelled the city – the republic's most important tourism resort and a UNESCO World Heritage site – in an effort both to scare away tourists and thereby damage the economy (at which they succeeded) and to destroy a potent symbol of Croatian culture and heritage. Now that peace has returned and independence been achieved, the city has been beautifully restored and tourism to it is being used by the Croats in their turn. The entry points of the medieval city bear plans showing the extent of the damage caused by 'the aggression of the Yugoslav army, Serbs and Montenegrians (*sic*)' with every building that sustained any kind of damage marked. The plans are littered with damage marks and the implication is of a near ruin whose magnificent restoration has all been achieved since independence. Needless to say, there is no mention of Croatia's destruction of the much prized sixteenth-century Ottoman bridge over the Neretva in Mostar, Bosnia, in 1993.

In fact, only 14 per cent of buildings damaged in the whole of Dubrovnik province sustained between 45 and 100 per cent destruction, while 19 per cent of affected buildings suffered below 5 per cent damage (Oberreit, 1996: 71–2). Many of the worst hit were outside the old city and still await rebuilding. But the Croatian Ministry of Economic Development, recognizing

Dubrovnik's unique charm for the international community, was (understandably) able to exploit this and gather donations for its restoration from governments, charities and individuals. Once more the city is a centre of beautiful buildings, good, fresh food and delightful classical concerts. It gives every impression of being one of the world's more civilized places, almost erasing the memory that Croats, as well as Serbs, committed many atrocities during the Yugoslav conflict.

The influence of tourism

There is ample evidence, then, that tourism is shaped and used by external actors and events, with political actions leading to economic consequences and vice versa. But can the tourism industry itself shape politics and economics? The possibility was already evident over 100 years ago. When Thomas Cook and Son, now doing business in Europe and the USA, bought up the Vesuvius funicular, they refused to pay the mountain guides the £900 fee extracted from its previous owner. The guides burnt down the station and cut the line, but Cook called their bluff by closing the whole enterprise until lack of tourists forced the guides to negotiate. Cook was beginning to 'wield near-governmental power and influence' (Turner and Ash, 1975: 55–6).

While not normally so blatant, tour operators today can use the flexibility of the industry and the similarity of certain (e.g. beach-type) resorts to shift operations to areas offering the best tax incentives, the laxest building regulations or the cheapest landing rights. Mass tourists are normally happy to accept only those destination countries offered in the brochure, while vertical integration in the industry means that computer reservations systems (CRSs) automatically offer flights and hotels with companies owned by the same parent company. Thus the direction of tourism flows is influenced and pressure is put on governments with no strong indigenous industry to accept unfavourable deals or no deals at all. Such pressure can, but need not, be entirely negative. In 1972 the UK Tour Operators Study Group (TOSG) induced the Greeks to delay tax increases to hotel bills (Turner and Ash, 1975: 221), which was clearly not in that country's interest. In 1973 the International Federation of Tour Operators complained about conditions at the airport on Mallorca and were promised immediate action by the authorities (Turner and Ash, 1975: 221). Might this not have improved safety for all users of the airport? Also positively, the more recent late 1980s withdrawal of British tour operators from Salou and other Spanish resorts that were experiencing an outbreak of cholera forced these resorts to improve their sanitation and sewage disposal systems.

Peace in the time of tourism?

It should now be clear from our discussion that tourism both influences and is influenced by external events and actors. But is it also able to bring about or facilitate peace? The answer has to be no. If we define 'peace' as 'freedom from war' or 'absence of conflict', as the dictionary does, the case against is clear. Increased tourism to the Middle East has done nothing to prevent or attenuate conflict in the region and we have seen that tourists may become targets – intentional or otherwise – in zones of conflict. Mega-events have also been used for symbolic displays of hostility, for instance the US boycott of the Moscow Olympics in response to the then USSR's invasion of Afghanistan. The collapse of tourism in Cyprus in 1974 during the Turkish invasion and the bloody break-up of Yugoslavia, whose economy was among the most dependent on tourism, must surely lay this particular solecism to rest.

Proponents of the 'tourism equals peace' thesis have argued that peace may be equated with economic and social well-being and that the benefits of successful tourism management bring with them an induced desire for peace. Even if we leave aside the semantic difficulties with this definition (see Burkart, 1988: 254), the evidence is scant. Improvements in living standards do not automatically predispose people to behave peacefully. The First World War, for example, occurred at a time when living standards were rising for many in Germany and Great Britain, while Lebanon – the Switzerland of the Middle East as it was then dubbed – was both a thriving country and a popular tourist destination before the start of its civil war. Neither fact could save it. Again, Yugoslavia must give the lie to the theory.

Perhaps the best that can be said is that at least some of those who travel have had their horizons broadened and their understanding of the world enhanced by doing so, and have contributed to their hosts' understanding, achieving a degree of empathy between them. This in itself is a valuable lesson.

If tourism is not a force for peace, peace is, however, essential to tourism, as the effects of the Gulf war and Lebanese civil war described above have demonstrated. Just as tourism flourished during two centuries of stability throughout the Roman empire but withered away during the so-called Dark Ages, just as travel across Europe boomed after the Battle of Waterloo put an end to the Napoleonic wars, it is no coincidence that tourism has reached its current proportions over a period of unprecedented global (as opposed to local) peacefulness. Since tourists are so easily able to desert any destination that becomes embroiled in a conflict, we should perhaps view the industry, not as a conveyer of stability, but as a barometer of any instability, whether political, military or economic. In general terms, although tourist decisions as influenced by industry and government do affect destinations and people in the global political economy, tourism as a whole is dependent on that political economy for the form it takes. This theme will be pursued in subsequent chapters.

4

Tourism institutions – where do they fit in?

So far in this book we have looked at what might be called tourism's 'unofficial' relationship with international affairs, i.e. the ways in which events ostensibly unconnected with the industry may affect it, and how individual governments or businesses use tourism or attempt to shape its practice. But what of the 'official' collective organizations set up either to promote or regulate tourism internationally? How strong is their lobby or effective their writ, given the multi-sectoral nature of the industry and the large number of small and medium-sized enterprises (SMEs) involved?

It is worth noting that tourism has been far less institutionalized at the international level than many other industries, and probable that this is the result both of the above mentioned variety of sectors involved and of the unique nature of the product: an 'export' which never leaves home and forms part of a country's 'invisible' earnings. (At the national level, most countries have some form of national tourism organization carrying out research and marketing and/or a government department responsible for the industry, as well as Chambers of Commerce representing members of the industry.) Tourism was not included in

General Agreement on Tariffs and Trade (GATT) negotiations until 1986, when a decision was reached to apply the GATT to trade in services. Industry workers lack a single trade union through which to express their concerns, such as is available to car workers, miners or farmers for instance, instead having to join unions for their sector (transport, accommodation, retail, and so on). With the exception of international legislation covering the airline industry, there is very little supranational regulation of tourism activities. There is also virtually no likelihood of tourism producers forming an Organization of Petroleum Exporting Countries (OPEC)-type cartel. Since most countries of the world have some level of tourism industry and the remainder are potential destinations, everyone would have to join the cartel to make it effective, which would result in countries fixing prices against their own citizens as well as others. They would thus be hurting themselves as much as those others.

Nevertheless, this situation is beginning to change. Recognition of the importance of sectors like telecommunications and banking has led to the establishment of a GATS, in which tourism is included, and a number of regional trade agreements now has some bearing on tourism. Limited legislation has been enacted by the EU to cover tourism in Europe. The WTO acts to promote tourism worldwide. In examining the role and effectiveness of these institutions, it will also be argued that, rather than promoting or acquiescing to interests that are unique to the tourism industry, these institutions are simply reflecting current global concentrations of power. We will begin by discussing the promotional bodies.

Private sector institutions

While the focus here is on public sector organizations and arrangements, there are of course several private sector groups representing the interests of components of the tourism industry such as the airlines, tour operation and accommodation, and it is worth examining one of these in more detail first. The WTTC was founded in 1990 and is funded by its members, a coalition of chief executives of the world's major travel and tourism companies. As such it cuts across the boundaries separating sectoral interest groups such as the International Air Transport Association (IATA), TOSG and the International Hotel Association (IHA). As its first Chairman, James D. Robinson III, put it: 'WTTC is a truly global organization ... The members will focus on improving the quality and recognition of travel' (WTTC, 1990: 183). Its aims in this regard are to 'convince governments of the economic and strategic importance of travel and tourism, promote environmentally compatible development and *eliminate barriers to growth* of the industry' (Hawkins, 1994: 299, emphasis added). In other words, the organization is bent on expansion of tourism and does not appear to see this as contradicting its objective of making the industry 'environmentally compatible'.

We should not be surprised by this, however: in an increasingly competitive, profit-driven world economy, the only way to survive is to go on making more profits. This is exactly what all major industries – oil, car, chemicals and, notoriously, arms – do. The dynamics of the international system make it impossible for them not to. The WTTC has accordingly used public policy fora to convince governments of tourism's importance to national economies, producing a number of reports on the subject, and it maintains an office in Brussels (its HQ is in London), giving it close proximity to the decision-making centres of the EU.

The WTTC has also sent delegations to different countries, e.g. China, to discuss ways of improving their tourism. In keeping with its interest in the environment, it sponsored the creation of the World Travel and Tourism Environment Research Centre (WTTERC) at Oxford Brookes University, UK. The WTTERC's objectives are to design databases on environmental best practice and increase the amount of information on bringing about environmental improvement available to policy-makers, tourism companies, etc; to monitor the nature of agreements and codes of practice influencing tourism company programmes; to promote scientific research on encouraging sustainable development in the industry; and to build up case study evidence on the implications of tourism in specific environments. The WTTERC has now been subsumed by Greenglobe in the UK, while its data are disseminated by Econet, an organization jointly funded by the WTTC and the EU. While 'deep green' researchers may consider it misguided to assume that tourism can always be made environmentally friendly, there is no reason to believe that the WTTC is not sincere in its efforts, while remaining true to its desire to promote the industry.

The WTTC has been effective at creating a high profile for itself then. More importantly, it has contributed to raising tourism higher up the economic agenda. It was active in supporting an agreement on services during the GATT Uruguay Round: WTTC President, Geoffrey Lipman, met GATT Director General, Arthur Dunkel, in June 1991, when talks looked in danger of collapse, to urge their successful conclusion and present a report on tourism in the world economy (WTTC, 1991). As we shall see below, the Uruguay Round was subsequently completed (in December 1993) and tourism was included.

The public sector

If international industry groups behave in expected ways to safeguard their interests, are there any similarities in the way public international organizations conduct themselves, and if so, why? Let us turn to the WTO.

The WTO superseded the International Union of Official Tourism Organizations (IUOTO) and was created at an extraordinary General Assembly of that body in 1975. Lanfant and Graburn (1992: 95) claim that the IUOTO was itself first established in 1925 as the wonderfully, if improbably, named Union of Official Spokesmen of Official Touristic Propaganda. The WTO has been recognized by the UN General Assembly as the inter-governmental organization (IGO) with responsibility for tourism but it is not an official organ of the UN. It does, however, provide much of its technical assistance to developing countries in co-operation with the United Nations Development Programme (UNDP) (Vellas and Becherel, 1995: 260).

Membership of the organization is divided between countries which have ratified or accepted its constitutional statutes, of whom there were 135 at the end of 1997, and some 200 international NGOs actively involved in tourism, which are affiliated to it. Non-state territories like Macau can be associate members and the Vatican is a permanent observer (Vellas and Becherel, 1995: 258). The WTO's structure comprises a general secretariat, based in Madrid, a general assembly and six regional commissions, an executive council with four subsidiary committees, and the Committee of Affiliated Members, which is organized into working groups on youth tourism; consumer behaviour; investment; employment; tourism and health; and information technology (Vellas and Becherel, 1995: 259–60).

The goals of the WTO, as set out in Article 3 of its statute in language remarkably similar to the idealistic yet pompous phrases of many UN organs' charters, are to 'promote and develop tourism in order to contribute to economic expansion, international understanding, peace and prosperity, as well as to promote universal respect and the observance of basic human freedom and rights without distinction of race, sex, language or religion'. It does this via activities that include:

■ publishing global and regional statistics
■ publishing studies on world tourism trends, tourism markets, tourism enterprises and equipment, tourism planning and development, economic and financial analysis, sociological impacts of tourism activity, and representations of tourism abroad

- organizing training workshops on marketing, finance and land development, etc.
- providing developing countries with technical assistance, either from its
  own budget or by delegating the project and its funding to the UNDP
- encouraging international consultation among its various organs by
  proposing specific actions to its member countries and adopting resolutions
  and draft recommendations deemed important for the social development
  of tourism in its member countries.

Of the last, the most important is the Manila Declaration of 1981, among
whose main points are that:

- development of tourism from abroad should be accompanied by similar
  efforts to expand domestic tourism
- economic returns should not be the sole basis for encouraging tourism
- improved employment conditions in tourism should be promoted
- tourism resources should be managed and conserved.

The declaration also states that tourism is a basic need and that society has a
duty to enable its citizens to participate in it (c.f. Article 24 of the Universal
Declaration of Human Rights 1948, which states: 'Everyone has the right to
rest and leisure including reasonable limitation of working hours and periodic
holidays with pay'). It further declares that tourism 'is suitable for the
foundation of a new economic order which will narrow the gap between the
developed countries and the underdeveloped . . . a means to promote the
lessening of international tensions' (WTO, 1981: 5). Between 1980 and 1991
the organization carried out some 500 operational and sectoral support
missions, and 120 technical co-operation projects, spending US$17.1 million
in the process (Vellas and Becherel, 1995: 262).

It is obvious from the above that the WTO both supports tourism, and
strives to see that it is implemented successfully and with the most benefit for
all parties. Aid for developing countries, which make up the bulk of its
membership, has been particularly noteworthy. But it is also not difficult to
infer that, like the WTTC, the organization views the growth and spread of
tourism as inevitable and highly desirable, despite the large body of data
showing that, in excess, tourism harms the environment and can have adverse
social and cultural consequences. The mandate of its facilitation committee,
for instance, is to propose measures that relax administrative, customs, police
and health controls and make them more flexible in order to encourage
tourism movements across borders. In other words the aim is to encourage
more tourism.

Such a stance is hardly surprising but, for those who see tourism as predominantly negative, it could be considered an example of the way in which the (largely Western) industry is manipulating the global system for its own ends. I do not think it is that simple. Rather, just as the major international organizations (IOs) set up at the end of the Second World War – the Bretton Woods financial institutions, the UN and its various organs – were tailored to suit the historical circumstances prevailing at the time (a triumphant USA allied to a small number of industrialized, colonialist states), so the WTO has reflected the changed but essentially similar conditions of the international system in the 1970s. The earlier IOs were all located in the West (most of them in the USA) and had their charters drawn up by Western officials with an eye on maintaining their interests. The earliest proposals for UNESCO's constitution, for instance, were drafted by a US panel of experts and gave prominent billing to the free flow of information (Schiller, 1976: 34), a doctrine the USA knew would be beneficial to its free market economy.

The WTO is also sited in the West (Spain) and the commitment to economic growth emphasized in Article 3 of its statute echoes the dominant economic paradigm of 'the market', allowing capital the freest possible movement and encouraging pursuit of the greatest possible profit. By contrast, its more recent emphasis on the non-economic aspects of tourism, on the need to conserve assets and encourage tourism for all (these last two potentially in tension) mirrors the demands for greater equity in all spheres of economic activity that began to be voiced by formerly colonized 'Third World' countries in the late 1970s, right down to the phrase 'new [international] economic order'.

International agreements

How far these countries have been successful in securing greater benefits for themselves from tourism is open to debate – many would say that progress has been poor. But what we can say clearly is that, once again, tourism has proved to be a barometer of the way the international political economy is organized, something that is also evident in its inclusion in the GATS and other trade agreements, to which we shall now turn.

The status of tourism in these agreements reflects two long-standing trends. One is the general neglect of the industry at the international level. The fragmentation of the industry has already been discussed, as has its image as 'not quite serious' in the eyes of many governments. For example, the USA which, given its size and the variety of its landscapes, climate and attractions, has a potentially world-beating 'product', has no coherent national tourism policy – to the relief of many European governments, firms and National

Tourist Offices (NTOs) no doubt. But the latter would also be the first to complain about the EU's lack of any overarching strategy for tourism. In trade policy terms this has resulted in tourism being included in agreements almost by default. There is no special chapter or article covering tourism in the North American Free Trade Agreement (NAFTA) – though it had its own sectoral annex in the earlier Free Trade Agreement between the USA and Canada – and the implications for it arise out of more general provisions on investment, trade in services and temporary entry. A similar situation is evident in the Closer Economic Relations (CER) agreement between Australia and New Zealand, where it receives a passing reference in the preamble and is assumed to be part of the Protocol on Trade in Services because it does not appear on the 'negative list' of areas excluded from the agreement. There are, in fact, few barriers to the expansion of trans-Tasman tourism (Pearce, 1995: 115) barring the lack of a single aviation market. This *was* to be addressed by the agreement but was treated more as a transport matter (Pearce, 1995: 114). The provisions of the single aviation market agreement were unilaterally suspended by Australia in 1994 in advance of the public flotation of Qantas Airlines (Pearce, 1995: 120) but the agreement was eventually signed in September 1996 and came into force in November of that year.

The other trend is the ongoing and apparently inexorable integration of the world economy through deregulation, e.g. of the airline industries in Europe and the USA, and through the removal of tariff and non-tariff barriers to trade and, in particular, the implementation of 'national treatment', allowing companies to operate abroad on the same terms as domestic companies. After years of neglect, tourism has become part of the project to incorporate all economic activity into a global system. Tourism is specifically incorporated in the GATS therefore, under 'Tourism and Travel Related Services', which covers hotels and restaurants; travel agencies and tour operators' services and tourist guides' services. Entertainment, museums and sports are also covered under 'Recreational, Cultural and Sporting Services'.

What are the benefits to be gained from incorporating tourism into trade agreements? For countries, trade liberalization in general is thought to promote healthy competition, exports, job creation and thus economic growth. By removing restrictions on tourism trade, the same should occur in the tourism industry, it is believed. Regional agreements also offer the possibility for joint marketing campaigns, say between Australia and New Zealand, or, in the case of NAFTA, for strengthening the individual parties – the USA, Canada and Mexico – in the face of competition from Europe and Asia.

For tourists themselves, there is the probability of lower air fares where single aviation markets are created and lower prices in other areas thanks to the competition which free trade is supposed to foster; easier and less time-consuming movement between countries through the relaxation of visa restrictions and passport controls or creation of single entry destinations (permitting passengers to clear customs for more than one country at one port of entry, as has been mooted between Australia and New Zealand); and, potentially, higher standards in hotels owned and run by experienced foreign operators.

This latter point obliquely illustrates the main benefit for tourism businesses: market access for foreign suppliers of services and non-discriminatory treatment of foreign subsidiaries. Thus, under NAFTA, US and Canadian tourism companies wishing to invest or run services in Mexico may do so on the same terms as Mexican companies. In theory, Mexican businesses can do the same in the USA or Canada but, in reality, their lack of resources and experience *vis-à-vis* the industry in these two countries will make it hard for them to compete. (Moreover, in a curious denial of free trade, the USA has not granted Mexican air carriers the right to carry passengers between the USA and Canada [Rodriguez and Portales, 1994: 321].) This pattern is likely to be repeated around the world, giving firms from the industrialized countries increased chances to dominate tourism in developing countries, albeit at the same time as providing the latter with investment monies, stimulating (low-level?) employment and increasing professionalism and technology transfer (Rodriguez and Portales, 1994; Smith, 1994).

That penetration of their markets and the extinction of local firms might seem to the developing countries too high a price to pay for foreign exchange has been acknowledge by the GATS. Among a list of obligations and disciplines contained in its Articles, are 'modalities for *increasing the participation of developing countries* in world trade services (Handszuh, 1992: 264, original emphasis). Its application to tourism is explained as follows:

> In the case of developing countries their abundant tourism resources do not necessarily translate into the ability to generate and retain the value-added in a situation where the distribution machinery and ground facilities are owned and operated from within the tourism generating countries. While removing any doubt regarding the legitimacy of measures taken by developing countries to strengthen their domestic services capacity . . . this provision enables them to attach conditions to access, e.g. minimum *requirements for training and employment* in

39

foreign-owned hotels, *surcharges and different tax rates, access to technology,* or *access to distribution channels and information networks.*

(Handszuh, 1992: 264–5, original emphasis)

Here again then we see tourism following where others have led. As neoliberalism spreads across the globe the conditions created are facilitating the implementation of tourism – at least for some – and it is gradually being seen as an activity worth including in agreements on services. As developing countries have tried to lobby for greater equality in the terms of trade, concessions (some might say sops) have been made regarding the conduct of tourism in these countries.

Overall, though, the trend has been towards deregulation, as has been the case in so many industries, notably transport, health care and financial services, making it hardly surprising that there is so little supranational regulation of tourism. Only the EU, which produced the first major multi-country agreement on trade liberalization – the Single European Act of 1 January 1993 – has attempted it. It has taken the form of a Directive on Package Travel, a consumer protection measure whose key feature is a bonding and security regime to protect tourists in cases where a tour operator goes bankrupt.

No serious disputes or litigation have taken place since the directive became law in 1992 (Grant, 1996: 319) and it does not seem to have caused as many problems for the travel industry as was anticipated. In the UK at least outbound operators, who were already bound by an internal code of practice, have had few difficulties adjusting to it, while domestic businesses, especially small ones, have been able to remain largely ignorant of its regulations, thanks to the Department of Trade and Industry's failure to extend the licensing of air tour operators to all tour operators (Grant, 1996: 321).

If this suggests that international legislation is likely to remain a minor feature of the tourism scene, in keeping with increasing moves towards deregulation, we should nevertheless mention two possible countervailing forces. One is the growth of 'consumer power' (the Package Travel Directive was enacted to protect consumers), which could yet lead to the formulation of more measures to satisfy the customer's needs. The other is the paradoxical recognition that, in an interdependent world, regulation is now necessary in some areas from which it was previously absent in order to avoid complete chaos. The 'freedom of the high seas' has been severely curtailed by the 1982 Convention on the Law of the Sea and outer space is now regulated in terms of frequency allocations of the radio spectrum and liability for launch failures. If the numbers of tourists continue to grow as forecast, it is not impossible that agreements limiting numbers of travellers or time or mode of travel will have to be reached.

Moving on from our examination of the context in which tourism takes place, we shall now turn to its specific impacts on the environment, on economies, on societies and on cultural heritage.

Part Two

The Specifics

5

Environmental impacts

The aspect of tourism that has arguably generated most attention in recent times is that of its impact for good or ill on the natural environment, with most commentators suggesting that its effects are more often for ill than for good. Such interest is hardly surprising given the vast public attention attracted by the environment since the 1970s and the growing realization of the largely negative impacts that almost all large-scale human activity can have upon it. For, as in other areas, tourism development has reflected changes in wider attitudes, in this case to nature.

Changing attitudes to nature

The present-day love of and concern for the preservation of nature dates largely from the late eighteenth- to nineteenth-century European Romantic movement, which saw nature – particularly its wilder manifestations – as the sole repository of virtue, purity and wisdom, and was responsible for popularizing former 'no-go' areas such as Scotland, the Swiss Alps and the Lake District. Before that time 'untouched' nature, particularly wilderness areas and awe-inspiring features such as mountains or waterfalls, were regarded with horror, as dangerous areas to be avoided at all costs; at best a necessary evil to be endured, for instance when undertaking the Grand Tour. Daniel Defoe described the Lake District as 'the wildest, most barren and frightful' country he had ever seen. Even early Romantics were ambivalent about the power of nature, as the following description from an eighteenth-century guide to the Falls of Clyde in Scotland illustrates:

> A cold and fearful shuddering seizes upon your frame. Your ears are stunned. Your organs of vision, hurried along by the incessant tumult of the roaring waters, seem to participate in their turbulence and to carry you along with them into the gulph below ... Picture therefore, to yourself, the whole body of these waters with a din so horrid and incessant as to unstring your nerves and appal the soul, rushing over this rugged and abrupt bottom, into a dark and deep abyss.
>
> (M'Nayr, 1797)

In many non-Western parts of the world, this attitude still holds sway, for example in China, where nature continues to be regarded as dangerous and unpleasant – as indeed it can be if suitable clothing, protective equipment or transport are lacking.

Paradoxically, though, the other view of nature that dominated until the 1960s, and was derived from the Judaeo-Christian tradition, saw nature as a tool of mankind to be mastered for the good of humanity, a phenomenon whose resources, in the form of water, oil, gas, minerals and timber, would be endlessly available. The fact that the early mass market resorts were built with no thought for the consequences of the increased pressure on land, water and sewerage systems they would create was symptomatic of this general view that nature could always renew itself while still continuing to yield raw materials.

Now we know differently and this knowledge has combined with the Romantic veneration of nature to produce a distaste for anything that might alter the natural environment. Tourism, in its ubiquity, lies in the environmentalists' firing line and there is now a large body of work on the effects of tourism on the environment. Beyond citing a small number of examples to illustrate how tourism can both enhance and degrade it, the intention here is not to trawl through what is already well known. In order fully to appreciate the benefits and costs of tourism, it will be more profitable to examine how it compares with other industries in its environmental impacts and whether there are realistic, more benign alternatives to it as an industry. Further, we must acknowledge the conflicts of interest that cannot be avoided when issues of tourism, conservation, economics and social well-being confront each other: this may also help explain why tourism's impact on the environment is often seen as greater in developing than in developed countries.

Benefits and costs

Readers who do require a detailed account of how tourism can affect different ecosystems and different components of the natural environment (vegetation, water, air and wildlife) are directed to Mathieson and Wall (1982: 93–116) whose treatment of the subject is as valid now as when it was written over fifteen years ago.

Mathieson and Wall's (1982: 94) observation that it is difficult to distinguish between changes induced by tourism and those induced by other activities also still holds true today, particularly where there is multiple use of a land area. Nevertheless, it is worth recalling a few specific examples of tourism's positive and negative effects on the environment before we go any futher.

Continuing a trend started with the expansion of recreation, tourism can be credited with increasing the amount of land designated as national parks, game parks and wildlife reserves worldwide. In East Africa in particular it has helped secure a habitat for the region's teeming animals and encouraged locals to value and protect them. This in turn discourages poaching, as it also has in the internationally important Danube Delta wetlands, where recruitment of locals as wardens, staff at information centres and farm tourism hosts has provided them with an alternative and more sustainable source of income to their traditional, and more ecologically threatening, pursuits of fishing, hunting and smuggling (Hall and Brown, 1996: 52). Tourism has also been credited with allowing the Aeta, a negrito tribe in the Philippines, to preserve their dying way of life in its forests by running a Jungle Environmental Survival Training School for ecotourists (*Guardian*, 17 November 1997).

In the UK (and doubtless elsewhere) tourism and the money it generated was used to justify environmental conservation at a time when its importance was only beginning to be appreciated. Thousands of indigenous-style farm buildings and country houses have been saved from ruin or demolition by being turned into accommodation or entertainment facilities; their refurbishment often led to the saving of other buildings in the same area (Naylor, quoted in Burkart and Medlik, 1981: 249). The creation of country parks and long-distance footpaths in the UK also owes something to the demand from tourists and ramblers for greater access to the countryside (Naylor, quoted in

Burkart and Medlik, 1981: 249), so much so that tourism is now being considered a preferable alternative to the planting of giant coniferous forests in terms of landscape preservation and maintenance of biodiversity, as well as of employment generation (Urry, 1990: 99). In Austria pressure from tourists and tourism authorities was responsible for 'saving' the Krimml waterfall from being turned into a hydroelectric dam.

In stark contrast to this, however, tourists themselves are now causing damage at the waterfall because of pressure of numbers; various long-distance paths and mountain trails, e.g. the Pennine Way and parts of the Lake District in the UK, are also being eroded through sheer weight of numbers. Parts of the Himalayas suffer serious littering problems. At the other end of the transport scale, as well as causing noise pollution to those living near airports, aircraft produce carbon dioxide and nitrogen oxides which, while not affecting air quality at ground level, do add to the emissions thought to be responsible for global warming.

The influx of tourists to Mediterranean coastal areas frequently generates more sewage and other rubbish than local infrastructures can handle, to the detriment of marine life (and of the health of tourists and locals alike). In Goa, India, the problem is simply washed away from the exclusive tourist beaches and allowed to pollute areas frequented only by locals, while hotels receive preferential access to scarce pure water supplies (Noronha, 1994). The (often unwitting) activities of tourists have disrupted the breeding patterns of turtles in the Greek islands and Turkey, while promotion of diving has contributed to destruction of coral reefs in Australia and Belize. The presence of increasing numbers of people in 'wilderness areas' – trips to the polar regions are no longer uncommon – can be harmful to vegetation and wildlife as well as aesthetically and spiritually displeasing to visitors seeking solitude. Further aesthetic distress is caused when virgin landscapes become covered in unsightly buildings (or even sightly ones that are nevertheless out of keeping with the landscape in question).

The nature of the conflict

There is no denying then that tourism development can have severely negative consequences for the natural environment. But just what is a 'natural' environment? With the possible exception of the Antarctic, there is scarcely a natural landscape left on Earth, if we understand this to mean 'produced by nature'. For virtually everywhere on the planet has been shaped and changed to some degree by human (and indeed animal) activity. Soil damage in the form of swamping and salting was caused by the irrigation system of the

Sumerians as far back as 1000 BC (Wilden, 1987: 158). In other words, unless we are prepared to sit back and literally do nothing (thus causing the extinction of the human race), we have to expect that everything we do will have some effect on the environment.

Moreover, attempts to preserve it at all costs have led to some serious conflicts. The success in boosting wildlife numbers of many East African game parks has often been at the expense of local populations, no longer able to graze their herds in certain areas and banned from hunting in the parks. Thus elephant numbers in the Mkomazi reserve in Tanzania – established in 1988 – have increased from only two to nearly 1,000. The same is set to happen to rhinoceros numbers when a herd is imported from South Africa; correspondingly high numbers of tourist visitors will help to ensure their survival (*Observer*, 6 April 1997). In contrast to this optimistic picture, however, the Masai people evicted from the area by the Tanzanian government have seen their herds shrink, have experienced a severe increase in disease and malnutrition and are said to be on the brink of starvation (*Observer*, 6 April 1997). Increasing the number of animals can cause further problems outside the game parks too: elephants love figs and other subsistence crops and cannot read exit signs. It is a brave, nay foolhardy villager, who would try to shoo such a beast away from his or her garden.

A similar conflict has arisen in Burma, where plans for what its government has trumpeted as the world's largest nature reserve – to be partly financed by tourism – are being pursued in co-operation with the Smithsonian Institution and the Wildlife Conservation Society (*Observer*, 23 March 1997). Creating it, however, involves the removal – and allegedly the murder – of Karen tribespeople from their jungle homes, thereby achieving two of the government's aims: improving its poor environmental credentials and weakening a group that has long been fighting for greater independence. In these cases, then, the argument has become not 'tourism harms the environment' but 'tourism's support for the environment harms human societies'.

Elsewhere the protagonists may line up quite differently, as in the case of the Cota Doñana wetlands in Spain, subject of a bitter dispute for several years. Conservationists who insisted it must remain undeveloped were opposed by those wanting to build a leisure and tourism complex. The latter were not, however, from some foreign company, but local people enraged that outside (indeed often foreign) 'experts' should be telling them how to manage their habitat. From their point of view, their livelihood would be enhanced not ruined by the creation of tourism facilities. Such concerns are echoed in the row taking place over the plan for a funicular railway to take tourists up one of Britain's highest mountains, Cairn Gorm. Conservationists are horrified but the local community, for whom an extra fifty jobs have been predicted, is less worried. Moreover, it has been argued that, by replacing the main chairlift and by keeping passengers in an enclosed system, forbidden to tramp the summit when they arrive, the railway will actually improve the mountain's appearance and reduce pedestrian traffic (*Scotland on Sunday*, 16 November 1997).

To take a different example again, it has been argued (Donnelly, 1987) that, by banning or closely scrutinizing certain types of behaviour – beer-drinking, noisy parties, picking of flowers, use of motorbikes or snowmobiles – in national and countryside parks, authorities are biasing access towards the more affluent middle classes. Definitions of appropriate use have been made for and not by the users. Why should it seem shocking that many Thai visitors to their Khao Yai national park prefer to enjoy *al fresco* family meals accompanied by blaring radios, or to roar around on motorbikes, rather than walking the jungle trails as do the Western visitors? This harks back to the Romantic view of nature discussed above. Like Donnelly, Urry (1995: 139) has also noted that most professional opinion formers on the environment are middle-class proponents of the 'romantic gaze', i.e. one which derives from solitude and individualism. Their perception that tourism to the countryside causes congestion is not a problem for (working-class) adherents of the collective gaze, who, like the Thais at Khao Yai, value conviviality and sociability. There are thus myriad meanings of the environment and many competing interests (both human and non-human) for its use. They must all be borne in mind when examining tourism's impacts and those of other industries.

A comparison with other industries

If we think of the environmental impacts of heavy extractive and manufacturing industries, it seems less fanciful that tourism should be characterized as a smokeless industry (see, for example Soo Ann, 1973). The difficulty mentioned above of determining the exact causes of changes to the environment, and a lack of empirical data comparing the effects of different industries, makes absolute proof hard to come by. But no tourism-related damage to the environment can be compared with the destruction visited on the Aral Sea in the former Soviet Union (FSU). Once the world's fourth largest lake, large parts of it dried up and died in the 1980s after the Syr Darya river was diverted for irrigation purposes. The mining of sodium and magnesium sulphide along its shores has only added to the destruction.

Eastern European countries and the FSU, lands which until recently had relatively low levels of tourism, are among the most polluted in the world. The city of Kraków in Poland – a UNESCO World Heritage site – may latterly have suffered from congestion caused by tourists. But again, this does not compare with the disintegration of statue faces and the damage caused to metalwork and frescoes occasioned by the high levels of air pollution created by the Lenin steelworks in Nowa Huta and the Skawina aluminium smelter and associated lignite-fired power station located near the city, not to mention the sulphurous outpourings from the nearby industrial city of Katowice (mining and chemicals). It is no accident that the environmental arm of Solidarity – the Polish Ecology Club – was founded in Kraków.

Similar levels of poisoning, this time of land and water, are produced by the oil industry – the only one still to rival tourism in size – while the scars caused by open cast mining are at least as unattractive as those created by concrete holiday homes. Urgent attempts are currently under way in the US federal government to preserve the Great Staircase of Utah – an extraordinary rockscape of natural bridges, canyons and 1,000-foot-high 'stairs' – against those who would drill for oil and mine for coal. Interestingly, since visitors to the area's parks have increased by 300 per cent in the past ten years, tourism is seen as the only way of preventing this (*Observer*, 12 October 1997).

Even agriculture, as it is currently practised, offers no benign solution to the problems of pollution. Intensive farming has been responsible for soil and water pollution through the use of artificial fertilizers and of irrigation on a scale the Sumerians could not have dreamt of, for air pollution when crops are sprayed with pesticides and herbicides and for destruction of habitat through the grubbing up of hedges and the draining of wetlands. Using fire to clear land for farming also contributed to the massive smog from out-of-control forest fires that engulfed much of Southeast Asia in September 1997. The opening up of inaccessible areas by the logging industry has also contributed to congestion of wilderness areas. (For an interesting case study on the conflicts between loggers, resident anglers and tourism outfitters aiming to restrict numbers to Northern Ontario, see McKercher, 1992.)

What about the textile industry? This has often been presented as a possible substitute for tourism in developing countries (in, e.g. Shivji, 1973) and at first sight it is much more benign. However, except in the regrettably small organic sector, cotton and other natural fibre crops are currently drenched in pesticides as they grow and are often bleached during processing, with consequent pollution of air and soil (and damage to the health of industry workers, who are frequently not provided with protective clothing).

It might reasonably be objected that there is more to industry than the extraction, refining and processing of raw materials. Indeed, the trend worldwide has for several years been away from heavy industry and towards value-added and service sectors like telecommunications. This and industries like banking, insurance and computing have a far lower environmental impact (though they are heavy users of paper and electricity) and are less intrusive than tourism – are they not a viable alternative to it? Of course not. Not everybody is cut out to be a banker or computer programmer; moreover, these industries are not evenly distributed, either among countries (the vast majority are in the industrialized countries) or within them, being largely absent in rural areas. Thus such industries do not provide a viable alternative in many parts of the industrialized world, let alone in the developing world.

While heavy industry has declined in the industrialized countries, it has not vanished altogether. Humans do, after all, still need food, goods and energy, as well as information, in order to live. Rather, as the global economy has integrated, manufacturing has shifted southwards, to countries where wages are lower (and environmental controls often non-existent). Critics can rightly cite many examples of tourism riding roughshod over the environment in the developing world. But how much more hideous are the pollutant effects of the *maquiladora* factories in the northern border region of Mexico. Their toxic discharges have caused serious public health problems (Carruthers, 1996: 1008–9), turning the town of Tijuana into a virtual open sewer. Tourism may cause congestion, and untreated sewage from hotels is clearly a health hazard, but it does not pose the kind of threat to public health common to many other industries. Viewed this way, tourism does appear environmentally a more attractive alternative. Given that people in areas of industrial decline in the North still have to make a living, it represents one possibility that will cause less environmental damage than previous industries. For countries in the South, it could be the lesser of two industrial evils.

Conclusion

To continue to play off the environmental outrages wrought by tourism against those (much worse!) caused by many other industries would be unedifying. The point is not that tourism does not cause environmental damage – it does; nor that other industries may make matters worse – they do. The point is that, in a global system that values profit above all else, where companies can only remain in business by seeking constantly to lower their production costs, the environment is bound to suffer. Mathieson and Wall's (1982: 113) remark that the negative physical effects of tourism are mostly the result of inadequate planning is as true for any other industry. But planning will not come first if survival depends on profit. If we accept that there is an unequal balance of power in the global political economy, it is understandable that negative environmental effects should be greatest in the developing world.

For at first sight such an assertion seems strange: the industrialized countries receive many more tourists than do the developing countries. New Lanark in Scotland receives in one month roughly the same number of visitors that Albania does in a year, for instance, while tourists to Spain's beaches far outnumber those visiting the sands of Thailand and Turkey combined. In these latter countries, however, planning controls are considerably weaker than in the West. Those impacts which can be avoided or mitigated by controls are thus left unchecked, not because Third World governments care less about their countries (though corruption does exist as it does everywhere), but because, where power is shared unequally and options are few, the ability to lay down conditions for investment is limited.

When thinking about the environmental impacts of tourism then, it is not enough to consider them in a vacuum. First, they have to be balanced against the effects produced by other industries and the fact that all productive activity – without which humans cannot live – creates some environmental modifications. Second, environmental considerations have, at least in some situations, to be traded off against human needs. The relationship between tourism, conservation, the economic and social well-being of host populations and the leisure needs of different sections of society (both visitor and visited) is not clear cut. Backpackers on a limited budget who seek out-of-the-way places obviously do less environmental damage than would a mass tourist resort, but they contribute virtually nothing to the local economy. And in their drive to reach the unspoilt before everybody else, they are paving the way for later mass development of the very areas that may be least environmentally able to cope with it. Kathmandu, for example, one of the top 'hippy' destinations of the 1970s is now increasingly being visited by mainstream tourists. Without budget travellers' 'pioneering' (Pryer, 1997) activities it might still lie outside the tourist circuit. What is good for the environment might be good also for local people in one area, but disastrous in another. In a third it might close off already limited recreation opportunities to potential user groups.

Finally, the reason that such difficulties occur must be sought outside the confines of tourism, in the organization of the global system. It should now be becoming evident that, just as the physical impact of tourism can not be divorced from the impacts of other industries, so the environment itself cannot be isolated from other factors in the political economy. It was emphasized in Chapter 2 that social relations result from a fusion of the political and economic. Thus we need also to accept that tourism's costs and benefits arise from the totality of its impacts. With this in mind we shall move on to a discussion of its impact on economics and employment.

Just before doing so, however, we should perhaps end by suggesting that the environmental situation is not as doom laden as it may have seemed. Environmental impact assessments (EIAs) are beginning to be carried out in advance of tourism (and other industrial) development (though how far their findings are taken into account may still be a matter of concern). Further, in at least some resorts that have suffered environmental damage, attempts are being made to clean up the mess. Benidorm, the epitome of the package holiday resort, has won praise for the cleanliness of its beach and bathing areas, while Majorca instituted controls on hotel height and type in 1985, as well as introducing pedestrianization and traffic-calming measures and a programme for the creation of green spaces (Morgan, 1991: 17–18). Steps have also been taken to deal with the problem of algae on Italy's Romagna Riviera (Becheri, 1991). Actions carried out in preparation for the 1992 Winter Olympics in the French Alps actually reduced some of the impacts caused by earlier tourist and other development (May, 1995: 274). And big business/high-technology industries do not always triumph over rural lobbies, as an example from another sector shows. In Japan, the country's space industry has been limited to launching its satellites during two two-month periods per year only – in order to minimize damage to the marine environment offshore from its Tanegashima launch site – as the direct result of lobbying from local fishermen. These improvements may seem minor in the face of the number of serious problems that currently exist, but they show that not all environmental change is irreversible. Indeed, where change is concerned, the environment, which obviously conditions the types of tourism developed around the world, could fight back: tourism itself may be affected by global warming. This will be considered in the final chapter of the book.

6 Economic and employment impacts

As with the environment, much effort has been devoted to recording the economic impacts of tourism and its effects on employment. Indeed, it was the potential economic benefits of tourism that first attracted the attention of researchers and this remains the most fully investigated area of the tourism phenomenon. Young (1973) was one of the first to point out that tourism development could also incur costs, in terms of lost opportunities to establish other industries and of the creation of external (often non-monetary) costs.

The literature on tourism's economic impacts is even larger than that on the environment and, as with the previous chapter, there seems little merit in providing an exhaustive regurgitation of others' well-known material. We will content ourselves with a brief exposition of the main points of each side of the argument before posing two questions of rather more pertinence to the debate on benefits and costs:

1 Are there other industries which provide a greater benefit than tourism in terms of employment and income generation and are they appropriate for tourism regions?

2 Can the economic disbenefits of tourism, particularly those in developing countries, be mitigated, or is the way tourism is run constrained by the present organization of the global political economy?

Pros and cons

There are a variety of potential economic benefits of tourism, which are summarized below (see also Eadington and Redman, 1991; Archer and Cooper, 1994: 75–8). Tourism provides a major source of foreign exchange (particularly important for countries with non-convertible currencies) and thereby contributes to a country's balance of payments. Its status as an (invisible) export is suited to an era in which trade is seen as increasingly important, and certain developing countries – notably those in East Asia – have industrialized and modernized through export-led growth. In 1988 tourism receipts made up 25 per cent of all exports for Spain and 38 per cent for Cyprus (Witt, 1991).

Tourism provides income in the form of tourist expenditure, which accrues both to those working in the industry and, through direct taxation, to governments. Income also accrues indirectly to industries such as construction, which are involved in the provision of tourism infrastructure, to governments in the form of indirect taxation from customs duties, sales taxes and revenue from state-owned or -financed tourism businesses, and it is spread through the multiplier effect. The multiplier effect occurs when a proportion of additional income – in this case part of the money spent by tourists – is spent by the recipients on goods and services. The vendors of these goods and services in their turn then spend part of this income on further goods and services, and so on. Because tourism directly or indirectly involves so many sectors, several of which (e.g. transport and catering) are also used by non-tourists, it is difficult to determine exactly how much income it generates. The WTTC has begun using a 'satellite accounting system' which attempts to separate tourist spending from that of others and to include income from jobs generated by tourism in other sectors. Using the system the WTTC has calculated the total economic value of goods and services attributed to tourism in 1996 at $3.6 trillion or 10.6 per cent of gross global product (Travel and tourism survey, *The Economist*, 10 January 1998).

This figure may be inflated and can certainly be contested (see, for example, Townsend, 1997) but it does give an idea of tourism's wealth-creating potential. In this way, and by the stimulation of infrastructure provision and of export expansion, tourism contributes to general economic growth. This may be especially important for those developing countries otherwise dependent on exports of raw materials, whose often low (world market) price they cannot control. Such growth, it is asserted, provides the engine for 'modernization', which in turn fuels more growth.

Like any industry, tourism generates employment: according to the WTTC, it sustains over one in ten jobs worldwide (Travel and tourism survey, *The Economist*, 10 January 1998). Because it is a labour-intensive sector, this employment can exceed that created by other more automated capital-intensive sectors. Thus in the Seychelles in 1991, some 22 per cent of all workers in formal employment were directly or secondarily employed as a result of tourism – the highest proportion for any sector in the country (Archer and Fletcher, 1996: 42). Where tourism is developed in declining rural areas, it may halt a drift to the cities and provide new growth to the area. Urban tourism can do the same thing in reverse, providing a focus for the regeneration and revitalization of run-down inner cities or redundant dockyards, as in Bradford and Baltimore, respectively. In this way, too, tourism becomes a means of balancing regional disparities within countries and can contribute to development that is sustainable.

Much tourism work is based in the informal sector, particularly in developing countries. While this is disadvantageous inasmuch as no proportion of informal workers' income reaches government coffers and cannot therefore be distributed among the wider population, it does at least mean that tourist expenditure reaches those workers rather than leaking out of the economy (see below). Indeed, because informal earnings are not included in official calculations, tourism's economic impact may be even greater than supposed.

Tourism also may foster entrepreneurial activity in related areas such as handicrafts production and in other sectors able to take advantage of improvements in transport and access made to facilitate tourism.

On the negative side, opportunity costs may be entailed when tourism is established, i.e. the possibility of creating other productive industries may be prevented by tourism development. Such costs can be associated with any industry, though it has been argued that, thanks to low wages, productivity growth is lower than the average in tourism (Townsend, 1997). More telling is the fact that high levels of government subsidy to tourism (through tax incentives, funding of NTOs and subsidies to airports) divert money from other industries and favour the tourist over the resident (Young, 1973: 137–8; see also Wood, 1996).

Much of the employment created by tourism is not just informal, it is also low skilled, low paid and seasonal, a fact which, as noted above, may depress economic growth in the wider region (Young, 1973: 115; Townsend, 1997: 183). The fact that women fill the majority of unskilled positions and only a minority of managerial posts, serves both to keep wages low (women habitually being paid less than men for the same work) and, because these jobs largely involve housekeeping, catering and serving, to reinforce an existing and unjust division of labour.

Particularly in developing countries, tourism can have an adverse effect on agriculture by drawing people away from the land and into employment in hotels, etc., causing a loss of traditional agricultural exports. This is what happened in Yugoslavia in the 1970s, when many people migrated from inland to coastal areas to work in their country's newly developing tourism industry (Poulsen, 1977). Conversely, imports of non-local foodstuffs deemed necessary for the tourists increase. At the same time inflation and a rise in land values, together with speculation by outsider investors, can price locals off the land altogether. If tourism completely undermines agricultural and pre-existing industrial exports, a country will be vulnerable to this over-dependence. For, as we have seen in Chapter 3, tourism demand is subject to often unpredictable economic and political events, and even to changes in fashion and taste. Much of the Caribbean is in this position.

There are external environmental, social and cultural costs produced by tourism, such as the overloading of sewage systems and increased traffic congestion (see Chapters 5 and 7). While not easily quantifiable in narrow economic terms, they should nevertheless be balanced against the economic gains expected. If measures do have to be taken to repair tourism-related environmental damage, this will incur financial costs probably not borne by the tourism industry.

Most damagingly, the much vaunted economic gains from tourism are frequently minimized by 'leakages' of various kinds. These are often at their worst in developing countries and occur when income from tourism flows out of the destination, or never even reaches it, because of high levels of outside ownership of plant and services; through the sale of inclusive tours, whereby a package that includes transport, accommodation, food and recreational activities is bought outside the destination from a (foreign) tour operator; when expatriate labour is used to staff hotels and businesses, thereby denying job opportunities to locals and again remitting tourist expenditure out of the destination; and where imports (of food, equipment and machinery) are required to meet tourist demands, thus negating at least part of the balance of payments advantages provided. It has been estimated that the leakage of tourist expenditure in Fiji runs at over 70 per cent (Britton, 1982), while inclusive tours to Kenya have been calculated to cause leakages ranging from 40 to 70 per cent (Akama, 1997). Tourism developed in this way has been characterized as 'neocolonialist', an example of the economic imperialism of the North over the dependent South. The Caribbean, again, is often presented as the classic example (see Pattullo, 1996).

Economic options

These then are some of the pro and contra positions regarding tourism's economic impact. If it is clear that, while tourism can provide vital and wide-ranging benefits to an economy, these may be harder to achieve than is assumed, or cancelled out by harmful costs, what is the alternative? As with the use of the environment, it appears that, in many cases, there isn't one.

The decline of heavy industry in developed countries discussed in the previous chapter has left many regions bereft, and demonstrates the dangers of overdependence on *any* one activity, not just tourism. Likewise, the increasing mechanization of agriculture and the elimination of some human tasks by robots and computers have drastically cut the numbers of jobs available. In such instances, the fact that many tourism jobs are low skilled may be an advantage: 'there may be no alternative for the individual place' (Townsend, 1997: 190). While other economically important service industries exist, many demand a high level of skill and training not available to all. One industry that does not is the car industry, which has been revitalized in the UK thanks to injections of Japanese investment and management practices. But cars are major air and noise polluters, while the figures of those killed and maimed on the roads each year speak for themselves – the external costs are massive. Just as researchers have emphasized the need to balance tourism's economic impacts against its environmental and social costs, so these must also be considered when evaluating other industries. Tourism can, at a minimum, provide income and employment to areas where old industries have been closed down, the land is agriculturally marginal and there are no nearby high-technology centres. Of course, not all such areas possess sufficient natural or built attractions, though the increasing diversity of tourism experiences sought – there is a growing interest in industrial heritage, for instance – may mitigate even this fact.

In the Third World, as we have noted, options are often even more limited and it is hard not to agree with Urry (1990: 65) that 'it has to be asked whether many developing countries have much alternative to tourism'. Prices of raw materials are unstable and usually low. Many developing countries, especially small island states, do not even possess such resources, while the export of cash crops – a system imposed during colonial times – does as much if not more than tourism to destroy traditional agriculture. Indeed, it was the prevention by cash cropping of an agricultural revolution, such as took place in the developed countries before the Industrial Revolution, that has stifled development in the South, forcing countries to import just to feed their populations. Although they are often seen as another form of colonialism, jobs in tourism are generally considered to pay better than those in agriculture and in some countries, e.g. Indonesia, income from them can be significantly higher than the national minimum wage (Cukier and Wall, 1994: 465–6). In addition, where destinations can encourage visitors to sample local produce (unfortunately, too many are resistant), tourism can actually support local agriculture.

Where textiles are concerned the picture is unclear. Shivji (1973) presents accounts of the economic impact of textiles versus tourism that reach quite opposite conclusions. What is known, however, is that pay in the sweatshop textile factories of Asia, where women produce garments and shoes for many of the big Western clothing firms – Nike has been a notorious example – is abysmal, as it is in many other manufacturing sectors, e.g. the *maquiladoras* which were previously in this book shown to be environmental disaster areas. Yet the goods produced sell for exorbitant prices in the West – at least £50 for a pair of trainers. It should be quite obvious then that 'high leakages . . . [and external costs] . . . are common to many forms of modernization in developing countries' (Mathieson and Wall, 1982: 62). This does not excuse poor conditions in the tourism industry, but it puts them into a wider perspective which will be discussed below.

The point again is not that tourism is an economic panacea but that, as economic relations are currently structured, and taking account of the shifts and changes in industrial production, it is at least no worse than anything else and does present an option where other resource-intensive or high-technology industries are precluded. Its unequal impacts are common to most current economic activities.

It is not helpful to argue that countries should not take the road to tourism development without suggesting any alternative, especially since the gradual formation of a world economy has made autarky an impossibility. There is one other industry, however, which looks capable of providing developing countries with considerable growth: the illegal drugs trade. The drugs industry is interesting not only because it has a number of parallels with tourism, but also because, although it operates outside any formal or institutional framework, it replicates capitalist forms of production and social relations.

For obvious reasons, statistics on it are hard to come by, but the trade in illegal drugs has been estimated to be worth between $180 billion and $300 billion annually (Falco, 1996: 131), which puts it in a similar league to tourism. Both industries also deal to some extent in dreams of escape, with a pleasure product that is used recreationally to enhance the consumer's well-being. (Government agencies will never curb drug use until they admit this simple truth, which does not contradict the fact that addiction frequently leads to misery.) Just as almost anywhere can be turned into a tourist destination, cannabis, opium poppies and coca plants will grow almost anywhere in the world except the polar regions, making them ideal candidates for cultivation in developing countries for whom tourism may have been the only other option. Being labour-intensive crops they can generate a high level of employment and, because of their high exchange value among users, growers can earn more from them than from 'legitimate' crops, as many UN crop substitution schemes have discovered to their cost. For example, in Bolivia an acre of coca yields roughly $475 per annum, compared with a yield of only $35–250 per annum for bananas or grapefruit (Falco, 1996: 126). While governments and hence public agencies cannot (at least openly) take a share of the revenue because of the illegal status of the trade, there have been instances of wealthy dealers in South America using part of their profits to fund schools and hospitals. After all, they can certainly afford to.

But would we really want to promote an industry where not only are the revenue – and risks – grossly unfairly distributed, but where many consumers also suffer grievously? Many (not all) hard drug users suffer financial and physical degradation if they are unable to regulate their use, and may commit crimes in order to fund their addiction. Drug growers and smugglers see relatively little of the vast profits made – these accrue instead to the outside interests at the top of the supply chain – and pursuit of these profits which, as mentioned above, almost completely bypass government coffers, generates sickening levels of violence. Nevertheless, in the division of labour, the poor pay of the workers and the ruthless competition at the top of the supply chain, there are echoes of the way much legal economic activity is organized. It is to this and to our second question that we must now turn.

Organizational constraints

Could the economic drawbacks of tourism in fact be mitigated or its benefits enhanced if it were differently organized? Theoretically, this seems entirely possible. Let us imagine sub-tropical island X which, along with a wealth of beaches, forests and some arresting architecture, also boasts plentiful supplies of fruit, vegetables, fish and game and, in one bay only, significant reserves of oil. The island is able to finance the import of materials and skills necessary to produce a tourism infrastructure of hotels, airport, sewage and water treatment plants from its oil profits. Part of these profits is used to send its nationals abroad to be trained in hotel and business management. Upon their (legally required) return, these managers are encouraged to recruit staff from the local population. Although tourists arrive on foreign-owned airlines, the government has bought shares in one of these and charges high landing rights. Tourists are fed local produce. The government income derived from tourist spending is allocated partly to maintaining the tourism infrastructure but also to funding pollution controls for the oil industry, to establishing a small factory for the production of fish glue and fertilizer, and to extending the capital's main hospital.

This admittedly Utopian-sounding example does demonstrate that there is no intrinsic reason why tourism cannot be implemented to avoid major leakages and confirms Harrison's (1992: 17) assertion that 'the extent of [tourism's] contribution varies according to the area in question, any available alternative strategies, and the willingness and ability of government to create an environment for investment and encourage backward linkages with other sectors of the economy'.

In other words, it is all about options. For a country with a variety of potential income sources, or a scarce or sought after resource, or for one that is relatively self-sufficient, tourism can either form part of a balanced economic approach or can be ignored altogether. Thus tourism is only one of several sectors in most Western countries. Aided by its mountainous location, Bhutan, though a poor country, is able to severely restrict tourist numbers – and charge visitors dearly ($200 per day) – because the Bhutanese already have the essentials of life, as they (or perhaps more correctly their king) perceive them. And in the oil-rich Gulf states tourism is virtually non-existent – they have more than enough income and employment already (indeed, they are importers of labour). The Gulf states give the lie to economists' assertions that, without tourism, they are turning their backs on development.

But of course, many countries do not enjoy these options: it is precisely a lack of alternatives that has made them choose tourism in the first place. Where developing countries are concerned, they often do not have the capital themselves to finance establishment of the industry. In this case it is inevitable that foreign investors must be sought and understandable that the latter would expect to gain from their investment.

So as well as being about options, it is also about power and control. In other words, the *economic* impacts of tourism are conditioned by *political* issues. Together they create the social relations which characterize not only tourism but all industries (see Chapter 2). This is why it is necessary to examine the wider political economy if consideration of tourism's negative economic impacts is to have any meaning.

Dependency critiques

To be fair, some researchers have done this, at least with respect to developing countries, and have located tourism within the framework of neocolonialism, seeing it as an example of dependency. Dependency theory's best-known exponent is probably André Gunder Frank (1967), while Immanuel Wallerstein (1974) located dependency as a structural feature of a world-system. Dependency theory posits a core-periphery (Wallerstein), or metropolitan-satellite (Frank), economic relationship between strong, industrialized states and weaker states from whom the former are able to extract surplus and upon whom they can impose terms of trade to their advantage. This inevitably prevents economic advance in the weaker states and causes the gap between the core and periphery to widen. Frank goes on to argue that satellites themselves consist of a metropolis and further satellites, thereby highlighting the disparities within states and the role of local elites in the host economy, and building up a picture of a chain of linkages.

In tourism terms, although tourism may replace the cash crops such as sugar or pineapples exported in colonial times, since there is no change in the structure of the relationship between the countries providing the resource and those extracting the surplus (holidays), the relationship remains dependent and underdevelopment will result (see, e.g. Bryden, 1973; Britton, 1982; Erisman, 1983). Turner and Ash (1975) have even coined the phrase 'pleasure periphery'.

There is no doubt that tourism *and other industries* have been implemented in a way which brings far less economic benefit to many developing countries than it could. But there should equally be no doubt that the 'blame' for this lies largely outside the tourism industry and should be sought in the historical evolution of capitalism itself. In theoretical terms, tourism can be seen as an example and thus an illuminator of what has been a historical process of unbalanced development since the sixteenth century. Certainly there are destinations which fit the picture of exploitation painted by dependency theory but to castigate tourism uniquely is merely to shoot the messenger.

There are a number of problems with applying dependency theory to tourism. Where tourism has been developed in areas in decline in the West, i.e. satellites within the metropoles as Frank would have it, this is normally seen as a lifeline rather than an example of exploitation. Most empirical studies of residents show that, while there is often irritation at certain aspects of tourism, they would rather not be without it. Treating tourism as an intrinsically imperialist activity also does not explain why it is so important in metropolitan centres such as London, Paris or New York, which receive far more visitors than most developing countries.

Hall (1994: 124–5) has pointed out that the range of foreign tourism interests in developing countries is much greater than the range of economic interests existing in colonial times. This and the multi-origin sources of tourists make it impossible for one country to 'exercise a degree of control that could be accurately described as "imperialistic" or "neocolonial"'. He notes (Hall, 1994: 128–9) that island states in the South Pacific have begun to broaden their sources of tourism and investment to include Japan as well as Australia and New Zealand, playing off metropolitan regions against each other and minimizing dependence on any one source.

Even some highly disadvantaged groups have managed to turn tourism to their economic advantage. This is the case with gambling on Native American reservations. The Indian Gaming Regulatory Act of 1988 gave federally recognized tribes the right to conduct high-stakes gaming without state regulation in any state where (even just charitable) games of chance were operating (Long, 1995: 193; Carmichael, Peppard and Boudreau, 1996: 9). Many grasped the opportunity and have seen incomes and employment soar. For example, Foxwoods casino, run by the Mashantucket Pequot tribe in Connecticut, has become the largest in the world and employs 10,000 people; it had a sales revenue of $600 million in 1994 (Carmichael, Peppard and Boudreau, 1996: 9). On other reservations unemployment has gone from 85 per cent to zero (Rose, quoted in Long, 1995: 194). And on at least some of the reservations profits have been used to build hospitals, community centres and new homes with proper plumbing, as well as to create ancillary businesses (Long, 1995: 194).

This situation may be unique because Native Americans have total control over reservation land, giving them a degree of power they do not enjoy anywhere else in the USA. Moreover, many of the 'Anglo' communities close to the reservations have complained legitimately about traffic congestion and an increase in crime and, rather less legitimately, that they do not share in the revenue. In fact, however, they often do benefit economically through

7

Social and cultural impacts on hosts and guests

In examining the environmental and economic impacts of tourism it has become apparent that these do not differ vastly in kind from the environmental and economic impacts of other industries. They may be better or worse depending on geographical conditions or social and economic circumstances, but they are essentially comparable. The same cannot be said about tourism's social and cultural impacts, that is, its effects on people, their quality of life and their values, customs and beliefs. For tourism is unique in bringing the consumer to the product rather than the other way round. Producers of manufactured goods, and most people in the supply chain of services like telecommunications and banking, may never see the purchasers of their goods and services. Tourists, however, are seen not only by people who work in the tourism industry but also by others who may have nothing to do with it.

It is inevitable therefore that the presence of large numbers of tourists – many from cultures ranging in degrees of difference from that of their hosts – will have an effect on the societies they visit, and not improbable that they should in their increased retail sales and an upsurge in overnight stays. In the case of the Pequot casino, because the tribe is too small to staff it entirely with Native American labour, many Anglos have found employment there (Williamson, personal communication, 1997).

Hall (1994: 122) has also voiced another objection to the neocolonialist thesis, echoing Harrison (1992), who noted that dependency theory, like its counterpart, modernization theory, is a Eurocentric concept which frequently ignores 'the wants and ambitions of those about to be modernized' (Harrison, 1992: 9). Suggestions that Native American casino operation might ruin their 'traditional' way of life, which along with hunting and fishing has often tended to include alcoholism and extreme poverty, might come into this category. This is a topic which will be discussed further in the following two chapters.

Finally, recent global changes have called the theory of dependency itself into question (Leys, 1996). The rise of the formerly dependent newly industrializing countries of East Asia and the growing interdependence of the industrialized economies are examples. This has led Frank (1991: 54) to believe that, with the emergence of a world market, it is no longer possible to speak of national development and that development goals can only be undertaken by 'particular groups or classes' in ways relative to how world development affects the part of the world in which they live.

Frank's implicit conclusion is rather bleak in terms of whether the overall distribution of economic benefits can be made more equitable. It is echoed by Leys (1996: 56) who asserts that significant development is unlikely to be possible for many countries while capital remains unregulated. As far as tourism is concerned, we can conclude that, in the present condition of the world economy, like any other industry it is going to be more economically rewarding for some than for others and that the reasons for this are political. The real challenge is not to criticize tourism's performance but to use it to highlight developments in the evolution of capitalism both North and South – are there certain laws of capitalism which inevitably shape the way economic activity develops? – and to consider how control over capital can be re-established (c.f. Leys, 1996: 56).

turn be affected by these societies. Social impacts may arise from at least four different situations:

- as residents are faced with unaccustomed behaviour and demands from tourists
- as residents become involved in changing patterns of employment created by the tourism economy
- as visitors find themselves spatially distanced from their homes, in the midst of quite different ways of life
- as residents and tourists interact, both within and outside the context of the tourism industry.

Given that tourism has been associated with everything from a rise in crime to a drop in morals and from barring residents' access to or enjoyment of services to encouraging the homogenization and commercialization of culture, it is not surprising that most studies of the social consequences of tourism have taken a negative view of them.

Nevertheless, the subject has abundant grey areas and it is some of these that will be explored in this chapter. Since most studies have focused on the more easily observable effects of tourism on host populations, we will also ask how far tourists themselves have been affected by their experiences. Then, we will touch on the concept of 'authenticity', which is at the heart of much criticism of tourism's cultural impact and suggest that it is more problematic than has been acknowledged by those who wield it against tourism.

Causes of change

Even though the conditions in which tourism takes place provide immense scope for interactions leading to social change, such change is rarely provoked by a single cause and it is difficult to disentangle all the strands that contribute to it. While other industries do not bring consumers and producers into such close proximity, several of their products have had at least as much effect on societies as tourism. Advances in telecommunications mean that it is possible to talk to people all over the world and, increasingly, to reach them instantaneously through the internet. Western mass media and advertising have penetrated the four corners of the globe easily as thoroughly as has tourism. (A discussion of the large extent to which these media emphasize some events over others and favour reporting from the developed countries is unfortunately beyond the scope of this chapter.) The advent of satellite broadcasting means that programmes can be beamed across borders into people's homes without oversight or even permission from the receivers' government. Since there are more television sets than telephones worldwide (Dupas, 1997: 87), this is a powerful tool of propaganda (or education and enlightenment, depending on the circumstances and one's point of view). Improved communications and the economic shifts that have encouraged greater job mobility have also brought all sorts of people into greater contact with each other.

A transcultural survey of residents' views on tourism and its effects on their communities, carried out in seven countries in the 1980s, concluded that it was unclear whether the changes identified by respondents had been caused by tourism or by other factors (Bystrzanowski, 1989). This is perhaps not surprising since the majority of tourists still buy organized packages which limit their contact with local people to interactions with those directly serving them. But it also suggests that locals are more impervious to the effects of tourism than has been feared. In connection with tourism to a Turkish village in Cappadokya, Tucker (1997: 124–5) observes:

> It would be erroneous and arrogant, however, to assume that tourism plays more than a minor part in the identities of people who are not directly involved with tourists in Göreme. A few tourists walk past their houses every day of the summer, but there is of course more to these people's lives than just this. Moreover, there is a television in almost all the troglodyte dwellings, and images of a richer Istanbul-centred Other seen in advertisements and soap operas may have a stronger influence on their self-representations than tourism.

An Iranian spokesman on BBC Radio 4's *Breakaway* programme stated that, while his government feared undue Western influence from satellite television, it regarded tourists as 'innocent' (Radio 4, 10 October 1997). Tourism is, of course, currently at a very low level in Iran. More importantly, the government is setting the terms regarding acceptable dress and behaviour under which it takes place, a point to which we shall return later.

For the moment, however, we will emphasize what has been implied above – that many factors give rise to change – and that change can only be understood as resulting from this totality. Just as we have seen economic and social impacts either impinging on or resulting from environmental impacts, and vice versa, in the previous two chapters, it is important to acknowledge the interwovenness of all three effects. Note, for example, the economic motive behind the social phenomenon of job mobility. Note also that, as Valene Smith (quoted in Harrison, 1992: 10–11) has documented, economic benefits may be prized above adverse social and environmental effects. The inhabitants of the Philippine island of Boracay have endured the import of discotheques, drunkenness, drug-taking and prostitution, as well as pollution on land and depletion of coral at sea, since the advent of international tourism on the island. Yet tourism has also allowed young Boracayans to find work at home or to return to the island from the big cities, and they have enjoyed having cash with which to buy goods and services: most of them have viewed tourism very positively. In a further study, Smith (1992: 153, original emphasis) reiterated the multifaceted problems but concluded: 'Boracayans *like* and *want* tourism for social as well as economic reasons.' In other words, there are trade-offs to be made when seemingly adverse social effects are felt, and winners as well as losers in the social impacts game.

Tourists, tourists everywhere

We can illustrate this by examining two of the key areas where social impacts are felt: in the temporary sharp rises in population at tourist destinations which affect services and may give rise to the demonstration effect; and in the situation of women. While large numbers of tourists in concentration may create congestion and cause local services to be overloaded in one destination, their presence may also spur the provision of services that were previously unavailable to local people in another. Thus doctors' waiting lists in Llanberis, Wales, are always swollen by tourists in the summer months, causing locals long delays (Loveluck, 1989) but a Tyrolean village of 2,000 inhabitants that had been denied its own doctor on account of its low population, did get one after villagers argued that it was visited by 6,000 tourists a year (Oppitz, 1997). Similarly, it is doubtful whether my village in rural Scotland would still have even one shop, let alone two, for the purchase of a wide range of essentials as well as take-away food and video hire, if it were not for the presence of two less-than-attractive caravan sites on its fringe which attract large numbers of holidaymakers in the spring and summer.

Although the fact that beaches are sometimes placed out of bounds to local people (e.g. in Goa, Cuba during the Batista era and other parts of the Caribbean) has rightly been deplored, as has the replacement of essential food shops by souvenir outlets, it is important to remember that this need not be the norm. Tourism income can just as easily be used to support a much wider range of shops than would otherwise be available to local residents, along with a variety of leisure and cultural amenities. As was discussed in Chapters 5 and 6, infrastructural improvements to communications and utilities can also benefit residents. (It is ironic that locals who support the development of

69

'environmentally sound' tourism may find their hopes of improved facilities dashed on the altar of preserving the pristine.) The important question is who decides how the money is spent.

Visited populations, particularly in developing countries, are often thought to be subject to the 'demonstration effect', whereby observation of their visitors' usually greater material affluence and different ways of behaving causes changes in the residents' own behaviour (see Seaton, 1997 for a case study). The demonstration effect has been rather optimistically credited with aiding economic and social progress by encouraging people to work for things they lack. In practice, however, this can lead to a flight from the land (or even the country in an attempt to get to the West) and a change in consumption patterns that leaves traditional economic activities floundering. This is made worse where the use of land for tourism has caused a rise in land values that puts housing out of reach of local people.

More commonly then, and especially where locals are barred from tourist facilities, the demonstration effect has been accused of causing resentment and envy. Locals can see no hope of achieving the kind of wealth enjoyed by their visitors and this can lead to an upsurge in crime and attempts to 'rip off' the tourist. Thanks to the propensity of many tourists temporarily to mislay their inhibitions when on holiday, a corresponding change in younger resident behaviour is often observed, causing intergenerational conflict, while a misapprehension about 'foreigners' in general is created.

It does not seem from the above as if there are too many winners among local residents where the demonstration effect is concerned (and a tourist minus a wallet is unlikely to be a happy one). Numerous case studies have shown that tourism contributes to disruption in certain communities, although as was discussed above, the mass media have just as much effect. But the Boracay example shows that, at least in some cases, such disruption may be considered worth the cost, especially given the lack of alternative development opportunities. A belief seems to have arisen in some quarters that change is inherently wrong for 'traditional' societies and that local residents are hapless victims unable to judge what is best for themselves, when all they are doing is choosing a way of life disdained by their 'supporters'. Again, the vital question is, 'who is in control?' The Iranians doubtless have a firm grip on their nascent tourism industry; the Goans, with no other significant source of income and a less developed indigenous infrastructure do not (but see Wilson, 1997, for a revisionist view of tourism's impacts in Goa). There is no technical reason why facilities built for tourists cannot be made available to everyone, nor why improvements in water quality, sewage disposal, etc. spurred on by tourism cannot also be extended beyond resort complexes. Where they are not, this is the result of poor planning or of control resting with interests (usually but not necessarily) from outside the area whose chief concern is to maximize their profits. The fact that this phenomenon is neither limited to the tourism industry nor specifically created by it has been raised already. Its implications will be discussed in the concluding chapter.

And what about the 'political' demonstration effect? It has been suggested that tourism is supportive of right-wing dictatorships because of the industry's desire for 'order' (Turner and Ash, 1975: 185), a point that would seem to be borne out by the huge success of tourism in Spain after its large-scale establishment under Franco. But it is entirely possible that contact with large numbers of people from democratic countries helped pave the way for Spain's remarkably smooth transition to democracy and a more 'modern' way of life after the *caudillo*'s death. Surely this is the reason why leisure travel to all the most authoritarian Gulf states is banned: state leaders do not want their people to see the degree of personal freedom enjoyed in non-theocratic states. A similar state of affairs has been evident at the other end of the political spectrum: tourists to the former Soviet Union had their itineraries closely supervised by Intourist and were often taken shopping in foreign currency stores from which most Soviet citizens were effectively barred. In Albania it was virtually impossible for tourists to have any contact with local people other than guides and hotel staff before the 1990s. In North Korea, it still is. In Cuba, where locals do have contact with tourists, it has been argued that, thanks to their greater material affluence, the presence of tourists has provoked dissatisfaction, not with tourism, but with the government's failure to provide the same levels of prosperity (Seaton, 1997).

Women and tourism

Issues of change and choice come into their own where the position of women is concerned. As was discussed in Chapter 6, women's employment in tourism is often of a low-paid, low-status nature (Hennessy, 1994) which reinforces structural inequalities that consign women's work to the domestic sphere (Breathnach et al., 1994; Momsen, 1994). But such work has also suited some women, permitting them to remain in small-scale farming while supplement-ing their income from it, for instance (Garcia-Ramon, Canoves and Valdovinos, 1995). Becoming involved in non-agricultural labour has allowed others to develop entrepreneurial skills (Fairbairn-Dunlop, 1994), achieve economic independence and improve their status within society (de Kadt, 1979: 12). How far women's position is improved through tourism employment is thus at least as dependent on the norms and structures of the society they grow up in as it is on the structure of the tourism industry. And while many commentators bemoan the loss of authority accorded to (male) heads of families and decry the loosening of kinship bonds that have arisen in many Third World tourism destinations, this commentator is more inclined to applaud the weakening of patriarchal oppression and the liberalization of attitudes that had prevented women realizing their potential for too long.

The rise in prostitution that has paralleled the rise of tourism in many South-east Asian resorts and US and European cities, e.g. Amsterdam, and the establishment of specific sex tours, where men travel to have sex with young women, girls and sometimes boys, is definitely not to be applauded, but the idea that tourism has 'caused' prostitution is false. Cities such as Amsterdam, Paris and London have supported a thriving sex industry (including child prostitution, which was popular in Victorian Britain) for centuries. Sex tours to South-east Asia have built on indigenous prostitution based on local cultural attitudes to women, while in Swaziland prostitution has been shown to have grown up entirely independently of tourism (Harrison, 1994). In this case then, tourism may be considered not so much as a barometer but as a magnifier of existing social relations. The prevalence of prostitution in tourist resorts is a reflection both of local social structures and of the sexual attitudes and taboos that operate in the generating societies. The same can be said of the images of bikini-clad women and compliant, often Asian, air hostesses presented in some tourism promotional literature. They reflect much wider sexist and racialist attitudes.

Finally, in our consideration of the social impact of tourism on women, the opportunity for the better off among them to travel is another factor that has increased women's sense of independence and helped them learn to trust their own abilities. It is noteworthy that the majority of great women travellers of history, such as Lady Hester Stanhope, Isabella Bird and Mary Kingsley, used travel as a means of escape after disappointment in love or release from the confines of caring for elderly parents (Clarke, 1988; Hall and Kinnaird, 1994), though one (Isabelle Eberhardt) had to dress as a man to do so.

The shock of the new

The phenomenon of women (sometimes) achieving enhanced status through travel or tourism-related employment, and the fact that this may conflict with existing social structures, highlights one of the central problems implied by tourism development: the merits of 'modernization' versus 'traditionalism'. As Urry (1990: 59) has pointed out, 'some local objections to tourism are in fact objections to "modernity" or to modern society itself: to mobility and change, to new kinds of personal relationships, to a reduced role of family and tradition, and to different cultural configurations'. Three points, related to those discussed above, can be drawn out of this. First, it is not enough to seek the causes of social dislocation in the development of tourism – not only do other factors play a role, but the growing interdependence of the global political economy and the organization of its economic relations is inevitably drawing all societies, including the traditional, into an integrated world system. Tourism is but one means through which this is achieved.

Second, just as the question of who pulls the strings conditions how far the social benefits of tourism are enjoyed by host populations, so the issue of the changing family and gender relations attributed to tourism is also related to power structures. It is not surprising that, as women and young people begin to gain greater independence in rigidly hierarchical and patriarchal 'traditional' societies, those used to being in charge should object. This has been happening in Europe and the USA since the start of the women's movement. There are many unpleasant aspects to modernity to which we can (and should) object – a shortage of caring environments for children and the elderly, rising crime, the emphasis on monetary worth over more intangible qualities – but it is wrong to scapegoat tourism for them all without considering the wider context.

Third, change is not necessarily bad, even when it is painful. Change, after all, is what got us out of the Stone Age and, without the capacity to change, human progress would not have occurred. Why is it that, where tourists and those who migrate to work in the tourism industry are thought to have caused a change in values and customs, this is nearly always considered a bad thing? Why is the word 'incomers', which may include tourists who return to settle, virtually a term of abuse in some circles? One is much more likely to find bigotry, sexism and homophobia in small, closed communities – wherever they are in the world – than in large open cities. Kohn (1997) has argued persuasively that tourist, incomer and local identities may all shift over time, using the example of the Hebridean island of Coll, where former tourists who have settled on the island are viewed as essential to keeping services functioning and school rolls from falling throughout the year. Interestingly, both groups regard temporary tourists with a degree of ambivalence, even though the ex-tourists have come to be regarded as islanders.

Why also is it largely 'outsiders' who are the most successful entrepreneurs? Think of the overseas Chinese – chiefly responsible for the economic success of Singapore – whose communities thrive wherever they are established. This is not to suggest that all small communities are home to bigots, nor to deny the problems of crime and indifference to others that plague many cities, but communities that look outwards as well as inwards, with a varied social mix do seem happier places to be. Questions on the role and values of incomers should at least be posed. Although they refer to a much wider range of activities than tourism alone, research within the tourism context into which types of people are willing to leave their original home, which stay put and why could be a fruitful endeavour.

Impacts on tourists

Whatever one's view of the merits and demerits of the social impacts of tourism on host societies, there is no denying they exist. Much less attention has been devoted, however, to the question of how far tourists are influenced by their own experiences of foreign cultures. In the case of package tourists, contact is often minimal. Even backpackers, often depicted as boldly going where others fear to tread, can be a remarkably conservative group. It is possible to visit hotels in South America, South-east Asia, Istanbul, etc. known for their cheap rooms and find them full of Western youth all talking to each other, with not a 'native' in sight. Perhaps this is why so many brochure quotations of tourists' holiday memories concern landscape and nature.

Nevertheless, there are grounds for arguing that, along with mass media, tourism has aided the spread of aspects of different cultures to the generating regions. One example is the vast growth of wine consumption in the UK since the 1960s, and the relative decline in beer-drinking, which coincided with mass market travel to France, Spain and Italy, countries where wine is the preferred drink at meal times. Naturally, there are elements of fashion involved too, not to mention the marketing strategies of major drinks producers and supermarkets, but it seems probable that the spread of wine consumption from an elite to the middle classes in the UK has been facilitated by holiday experiences. Like the holiday itself it was originally seen as a status symbol and could be paraded in front of the neighbours along with the suntan to show that one had been abroad. The same may be true of tea-drinking at breakfast time in Germany. Another example is the more recent popularity of Thai restaurants in European towns and cities, which may be related to the rise in long-haul travel to Thailand. Further, not all the artefacts that tourists bring home are mass-produced souvenirs. Exposure to different artistic styles and to non-Western music while on holiday has undoubtedly influenced taste.

After all, there is a precedent for this. The eighteenth-century Grand Tour to Italy spawned an immense wave of copycat behaviour, with Palladian villas and Italianate statue-strewn gardens springing up all over the British countryside, as well as in Holland, Sweden, Russia and Germany. There was even a 'Roman Pantheon' built in London's Oxford Street in the 1770s (it burnt down after twenty years). Italian scenes were commonplace in painting and on fans and *objets d'art*, while Italian styles were copied for furniture and ornaments (Wilton and Bignamini, 1996).

Urry (1990: 58) has gone so far as to argue that tourism can indirectly aid international understanding: 'The shift in public attitudes in Britain towards a pro-Europeanism in the 1980s is difficult to explain without recognizing that some role is played by the European tourism industry and the way in which huge flows of visitors have made Europe familiar and unthreatening.' The 'tourism promotes peace and understanding' thesis was dismissed in Chapter 3 but, in this instance, I am sure Urry is right – the exposure to each other's country has created a shared understanding of European history and of the advantages to closer ties. Moreover, the cultural and material differences among Europeans are relatively small; many have had the experience of being both hosts and guests, so the likelihood of tourist–host conflict is minimized.

When tourists from the industrialized world visit the developing world, however, differences are much greater and more apparent and the potential for conflict correspondingly higher. We know about the resentment felt by some local people but there has been little attempt to study this from the tourist's point of view. How do women tourists feel when they are the object of attentions from men who believe they must be willing and available sexual partners? How do both sexes react to realizing they have paid double the going rate for a taxi ride or a piece of merchandise, or to the constant pestering to visit this shop, take that horse-drawn carriage or engage that guide? Tucker's (1997) study of tourism in a Turkish village noted that tourists were often suspicious of perceived over-friendliness of waiters and salesmen (*sic*), and sceptical about their motives, to the extent that they would more readily buy carpets or take tours sold or promoted by fellow-Westerners. Such attitudes would explain tour operators' and timeshare dealers' use of own-nationality representatives at the destination. Do such occurrences also colour future holiday choices? And if tourists are unfortunate enough to be robbed or attacked, do they ever wonder whether they might have provoked such behaviour or pause to consider what might have inspired it (e.g. poverty)? Would they be right to do so? These are all questions which would repay further research.

The tourist as hate-object

One other question also needs to be raised in relation to the social effects of tourism on tourists and that is: why are tourists so demonized – as much by academics as by host societies? This must partly be the result of their very visibility and ubiquity – they are easy targets of blame which obviate the need for probing more deeply into the origins of a problem and for accepting that its causes may be manifold. It may also partly be that, being in unfamiliar surroundings, certain character traits or attributes are highlighted. Ineptitude in a foreign language is not a problem 'at home', but it can be laughable, annoying or a potent cause of misunderstanding when abroad. Not understanding how a society works, especially for men brought up to feel that they must be in control, can lead to overbearing behaviour as a form of compensation. And, of course, being somewhere different can also fuel the desire to behave differently too. This is generally interpreted to mean getting drunk and seeking sexual liaisons, behaviour that might indeed lead to conflict. But it can also mean trying out a new experience – snorkelling, horse-riding, painting or even bungee jumping – and what is objectionable about that? In some cases, tourists may find themselves in a 'no-win' situation in which opposite poles of behaviour are both frowned upon (see Table 7.1). Could it be that part of the reason tourists attract so much vilification is because they are having fun?

Table 7.1   The tourist no-win matrix

Tourist activity	Too little	Too much
Spending	Seen as tight-fisted; not helping the economy	Resented for flaunting their relative wealth
Level of organization	Explorers, backpackers may be intrusive and a source of suspicion	Packaged tourists sneered at as herd-like
Interest in host culture	Seen as arrogant or patronizing	Credulous; candidates for ripping off
Interest in the environment	Seen as destructive	Seen as spoilsports, anti-modernization

Authenticity

The varied motivations that drive tourists to travel will be explored in more detail in Chapter 10. But we will examine one of them now because it relates to the consideration of social impacts in host societies. This is the (alleged) 'quest for authenticity' (MacCannell, 1976). 'Authentic' is defined in the dictionary as 'of undisputed origin or authorship; genuine' (*Collins Concise Dictionary*; *Chambers Twentieth Century Dictionary*). In tourism parlance, it may approximate to this meaning when applied to the production of artefacts, or to artistic performances or religious or folk rituals, to differentiate them from material produced solely for the tourist, with no heed of historical traditions. Already we are on potentially shaky ground, however, for unless such goods are deceptively described as, e.g. 'traditional Navajo jewellery' (and doubtless some are) they are not actually fake, they are merely new (and possibly inferior) art forms. Where they are falsely described, it is surely the tourist rather than the local who is being exploited. After all, Boorstin's (1964) contention that tourists – as opposed to travellers – actively seek out readily digestible 'pseudo-events', because they are unable to cope with the complexities of the 'real' world, has been widely dismissed as patronizing and elitist.

Instead, and more significantly, the notion of authenticity has come to stand as a shorthand for some sort of lost Eden, a premodern, untechnologized, rural society, which is contrasted with the inauthentic, industrialized, urbanized world (see Cohen, 1988). But in what way is this latter world 'not genuine'? It may be considered unpleasant to live in but that is not the same thing. Conferring the mantle of 'authenticity' on premodern societies by Western academics does not necessarily do them any favours. For, while it may provide a rationale for protecting them from (what these academics see as) the worst aspects of modernity, it may also prevent the establishment of desired improvements and help perpetuate structural inequalities. Just as it is not right to regard all change as bad, so it may not be helpful to confine the label 'authentic' to materials and events with roots in the past. We will bear this in mind in the next chapter, which focuses on tourism's impact on heritage.

Conclusion

But first, what can we conclude about tourism's impacts? Two points are worth reiterating. One is the way the boundaries between social, economic and environmental impacts become increasingly blurred the more they are examined and that developments which have a negative effect on one group of people may be matched by the privileging of other (perhaps previously disadvantaged) groups, and vice versa. Planners who wish to get a true picture of tourism's impact must consider the way all its effects contribute to a total impact.

The other is that the propensity of tourism to create good or bad social impacts depends variously on who goes where and on the factors – economic, political, cultural – that influence destination decisions. It depends on how the industry responds to structural changes in the world economy and, above all, it depends not only on who is affected, but also on who is in charge of who gets affected. In other words, we are back to power and politics. Although the impacts of tourism may be broken down into discrete units such as 'environmental', 'economic' and 'social', it is the way these impacts interweave and the way they are conditioned by political activity that determines their effect for good or ill.

8

heritage, the past and authenticity

The debate on tourism and heritage has often been reduced to whether tourism destroys or preserves beauty and whether it trivializes or revalidates culture. Needless to say, examples of each of these cases abound.

Pros and cons

Even the arch-demonizers of tourism, Turner and Ash (1975: 133) agreed that tourism to Turkey had – through the interest and appreciation shown as well as through entrance fees – helped to preserve the many Graeco-Roman and Byzantine monuments in the country, and if lasting stability should return to Cambodia, it will be tourist revenue (along with UNESCO funds) that finances the renewed protection of Angkor (Wager, 1995). Tourists' interest in arts and crafts has also spurred the establishment of institutes to train local artists in India and New Zealand, thereby revitalizing old art forms and creating pride in local heritage (Mathieson and Wall, 1982: 170). Similarly, in the south-western USA the presence of tourists has 'offered extended markets that served to heighten [Native

American] artistic productivity and to revive old traditions' (Deitch, in Sharpley, 1994: 151).

Tourists themselves have paid to attend holiday work camps for the restoration of old buildings in Provence, France (Boniface, 1997) and in the UK the public's willingness to pay to see 'stately homes' and gardens has allowed the old aristocracy to maintain sometimes crumbling piles while retaining a home and ensuring that architectural complexes stay in one piece. To some this might seem just another way in which the upper classes hang on to their privileges at 'ordinary' people's expense. However, Urry has pointed to the enormous support for such conservation among the latter. The National Trust, which looks after many of the historic buildings in the UK, is in fact the largest mass organization in Britain (Urry, 1990: 110). Such support, when translated into campaigns for the conservation of local buildings and environments, actually fosters local distinctiveness (Urry, 1995: 153). Finally, visiting a historical monument can provide a more stimulating way of learning about the past than sitting in a classroom; museums such as the Jorvik Viking Museum in York have been able to combine conservation with education and entertainment so that visitors learn something in an enjoyable manner.

On the negative side, there are examples of artistic effort being downgraded to meet tourists' demands. The marketing of Sri Lankan devil dance masks, and their subsequent mass production in styles and colours to suit tourists' tastes, has caused a loss of their cultural meaning and a drop in the social status of their manufacturers (Sharpley, 1994: 150). A similar loss of meaning occurred in the *Alarde*, a public ritual held annually in the Basque town of Fuenterrabia, when the authorities decreed that it should be performed twice on the same day in 1969 in order to accommodate tourist numbers (Greenwood, 1989). (The *Alarde* has nevertheless acquired new meanings, about which more later.)

Many 'art' cities, like Bruges, Salzburg and Oxford, suffer traffic congestion, fumes and wear and tear on their buildings thanks to tourists who come to visit their treasures (van der Borg, Costa and Gotti, 1996), while Venice has in addition suffered from tourism gradually 'crowding out' other urban functions (van der Borg, Costa and Gotti, 1996: 307). Venice, of course, famously had to 'close' on one extraordinary day when the numbers trying to get into it caused a complete jam. Wear and tear has also been severe at Schönbrunn Palace in Vienna, where the annual toll of 1.7 million visitors is causing the floors to break up. (Incidentally, when are those responsible for the management of historic buildings routinely going to insist that visitors remove their shoes in summer – as is the norm year round at temples and palaces in India and Thailand – and don overslippers in winter, as happens in Poland? This cannot deal with the problem of numbers but it does help to mitigate the damage caused by heavy shoes and high heels.)

In former Yugoslavia the use of tourism to foster pride in heritage has proved dangerously divisive where heritage has either been perceived as belonging exclusively to one group or has been used to suggest the superiority of one group over another. Although an extreme case, echoes of this are to be found in the much more widespread use of heritage to project a single, establishment-approved and rosy view of the past, which glosses over material hardship and political turbulence and frequently glorifies past economic activities that the present has destroyed (see Hewison, 1987).

Shades of grey

As with the other impacts of tourism, painting the situation black and white in this way is not fruitful. Just as it has proven impossible to treat the economic, social and environmental impacts of tourism in isolation in the three previous chapters, so tourism's effects on heritage need to be placed in a wider context. It is obvious that, if it is defined as 'anything that has been transmitted from the past or handed down by tradition; the evidence of the past, such as historical sites, and the unspoilt natural environment, considered as the inheritance of present-day society' (*Collins Concise Dictionary*), heritage will be affected both by tourism's environmental and its social impacts, while its packaging adds an economic dimension. As in other areas, conflicts are bound to occur among these spheres.

The commercialization of previously 'private' or 'personal' art forms may debase them in some instances, creating a social impact, but it may also provide the economic means for them to continue in others. As Hall (1994: 177) has pointed out in the case of Australian aboriginal art, its popularity with tourists and white art dealers has caused an irrevocable change in the way it is produced and viewed but, in the absence of alternatives, it is doubtful if the artists could survive without the income such a new form of production brings. The absence of alternatives is the key, for, as capitalism has become entrenched in the 1990s as the dominant mode of production, this has inevitably extended cycles of production and consumption – which means putting a price on virtually everything. As Turner and Ash (1975: 135) have put it: 'It seems safe to say that as long as the capitalist system lasts, it will continue to impose a commercial value on art and antiquities'. Tourism may be an 'ideal example' of the final logic of capitalist development (Greenwood,

1989: 180), but it is just that – an example. Tourism will not change on any great scale unless the whole capitalist system changes.

Tourism-supported environmental protection can also conflict with social considerations, as was shown in the case of nature parks in Chapter 5. Expensively maintaining a historical monument may not always be in local residents' interests if it occupies the only possible site for the construction of previously non-existent amenities. More gruesomely, some of the distinguished voices raised in protest at the shelling of Dubrovnik's ancient buildings had been strangely silent when it was only the people of former Yugoslavia who were being destroyed. Less bloodily, a desire to preserve buildings and monuments for future generations can result in an aspic-bounded site as meaningless as any 'show for the tourists', while denying access to those who would continue past tradition by conferring their own meanings on it. A prime example here is Stonehenge, where annual battles have been fought during the 1990s between police, 'travellers' and 'Druids' during the summer solstice. The modern-day Druids have marked this date at Stonehenge since 1905. Travellers had been holding a free festival in the field next to the stones since the mid-1970s. Growing numbers undoubtedly placed the site under pressure but, rather than relocate the festival further from the stones – as has been agreed for the new visitor-centre – the authorities banned travellers from holding it altogether. The exclusion zone placed around Stonehenge also effectively barred Druids from the site (Bender and Edmonds, 1992). In this we see a much wider conflict exposed than that between tourists and residents, one which pits 'the experts' against ordinary people and encourages distinctions to be made between appropriate and inappropriate use.

There may be sound reasons of conservation for a 'do not touch' mentality at some historic sites but I would argue that it is only by, say, walking on the top of Hadrian's Wall (discouraged but thankfully not yet prohibited) that you can get any sense of what it might have felt like to be a Roman centurion or a native stopped in her tracks. In the end, there seems little point in preserving monuments if they can only be gazed on from afar – in this way they lose all the meaning they had for previous generations. Why lament the fact that we will never see the Hanging Gardens of Babylon when – unlike the Babylonians – we have the Taj Mahal, the Colosseum, the Zimbabwe ruins, the Eiffel Tower (widely disliked when first erected), the Guggenheim Museum in Bilbao and many as yet unbuilt structures to appreciate?

Then there is the question of the replicas built to safeguard original sites from environmental damage while still permitting visitors to experience what they are like. This has been done, for instance, with the Lascaux cave paintings in southern France. One can argue, as Lawrence Durrell has done in connection with the Abu Simbel temple complex in Egypt, that moving or copying historic sites destroys their 'spirit of place', the atmosphere that makes them special. I would tend to agree; neverthleless, many people enjoy and learn from simulations (as at Jorvik) – if enthusiasm is so great that it threatens the original fabric of a site, such a compromise is probably the best that can be made, especially since interest in the past is now so much a part of life in the West.

The importance of the past

For this brief discussion should have demonstrated that tourism's impact on heritage, like its impact on economies and societies inevitably mirrors more general attitudes to change and to the past in the main tourist-generating countries. It is on this latter point that we shall now focus.

Like the concern with nature and the environment, to which it is related, the virtual obsession with the past common to the UK and, to a lesser extent, other European countries and North America, at first sight appears to be a Western phenomenon. 'Few Asian tourists trouble to visit the great medieval ruins of Pagan (in Burma), Angkor (in Cambodia) or Borabodur (in Java)' (Turner and Ash, 1975: 132). This situation may have partially altered in the intervening years as some people in developing countries have begun to travel, but the fervour for preserving everything from the past does not seem to have taken hold, as witnessed by the frantic construction activity under way in many Asian capitals. In Bangkok many buildings have been torn down in favour of modern replacements and most of its canals have been filled in. Moreover, there was no concept of purely decorative art in Thailand before the twentieth century, since all artistic production was a manifestation of the religious impulse (Hoskin, 1984: 6). In Lebanon the Ottoman villas that escaped damage in the civil war are now being destroyed to make way for new apartment blocks, banks and business centres (*Independent*, 26 November 1997).

Even Western reverence for the past is recent. Turner and Ash (1975: 132) cite the case of an Italian Baroque church that was converted into a car wash. Thirty or forty years ago there were no barriers at Stonehenge – I can remember as a small child wandering up and touching the stones – because visitor numbers were too low for them to need protection. In previous centuries stone from Hadrian's Wall was even taken by local inhabitants of the area for use in their own dwellings and barns. Nearby Lanercost Priory, a magnificent twelfth-century Augustinian priory, was built from Roman stone, while the great St Mark's in Venice was decorated with pillars and statues plundered from Constantinople. In these cases, the past was not expected to dominate the present but was used to produce something more appropriate to it.

Causes of change

What has caused the revision of attitudes? There are at least two related possibilities. One is the shift to a post-industrial, post-imperial, 'postmodern' economy in the West. The other is the West's position in the demographic cycle. As advanced technologies have made many unskilled and semi-skilled jobs redundant, and as even well-qualified workers find they need to retrain several times over their career, or have to work 'flexitime' or take part in job-sharing, old certainties about 'a job for life' and where one's life might be heading have been destroyed. Looking back to a past which we can know, rather than to a doubtful future, thus becomes more attractive, especially for those who regret the decline in political power demonstrated by decolonization. It is evident not only in visits to heritage attractions but in the use of reflexive neoclassical styles of architecture for current buildings, in the vogue for antiques and for past styles of interior decoration and in the sales of nostalgia-based magazines like *Country Living* in the UK and *American Heritage* and *Cowboy Life*(!) in the USA. The latter, it should be noted, is aimed at rich former city dwellers who have moved west and bought a ranch, not at working cowhands.

Even though such attitudes are most common in the West, they are not so much cultural as developmental, however. We have already noted that Western interest in the past is largely a phenomenon of the nineteenth and twentieth centuries and it accelerated during the postwar years as the pace of change – in technology, in reconstruction, in social attitudes – itself began to quicken and the Cold War created new uncertainties. It was doubtless also spurred on by the hideousness of much 1960s architecture and by the failure of town planning schemes and public housing to take account of people's basic needs for access to neighbours, shops, amenities and green spaces. The latter has contributed to the first exodus from towns to country in centuries. Thus the backward-looking conditions of which tourism is but one reflection lie in the evolution of capitalism, in economic and political processes.

In addition, late capitalism has, for all its uncertainties and upheavals, led to increased prosperity for a majority of people in the West (while a significant minority has become poorer). This has brought with it improved health care, including choice about whether and when to have children, and greater longevity, which have altered the demographic balance in the industrialized world. Most Western countries (and Japan) have ageing populations. Many of their retired people have an abundance of money and time, and elderly people typically like to remember the past.

By contrast most developing countries are, by definition, at a different stage of economic (and often political) development, and are located commensurately within the demographic cycle; since death control (i.e. the prevention of mortality through public health programmes and medical advances) is more readily embraced than birth control, they have much younger populations. Young people are generally much less interested in the past. Moreover, if the recent past is a colonial one, there is good reason to avoid looking back on such a period. But since most tourists to the developing world are from developed countries, it is often aspects of the past that they, on the other hand, want to see. Which brings us on to questions of power and control. Again tourism forms can be seen as a reflection of global processes.

Given the relative political and economic strength of the developed countries and the fact that it is their tourists who largely create the demand in developing countries, the likelihood of the past being presented as local residents might have experienced it is diminished. According to Hewison (1987), however, the same process is at work in developed countries, particularly the UK, where only versions of the past that concur with the ideologies of ruling parties are sanctioned at tourist sites. For example, the presentation of information at Stonehenge emphasizes the top-down nature of its construction, by focusing on the ruling elite, with no attempt to relate how ordinary members of society might have been affected by it (Bender and Edmonds, 1992).

Authenticity again

This brings us back to authenticity, for it provides an example of how authenticity is 'constructed' through marketing and interpretation (Hughes, 1995), which *ipso facto* should make it inauthentic in MacCannell's (1976) terms. Yet in this act of construction the tourism industry is only reflecting the wider fact that reality itself is not an immutable given but has also been constructed. As was argued in Chapter 2, current reality should not be considered a natural, scientific state of affairs but rather as arising from particular sets of social relations (c.f. Hughes, 1995). Urry (1990: 9) cites Crick's (1988) point that all cultures are invented, remade and have their elements reorganized in a process that is little different from the way events may be organized for tourists.

With this in mind, we can reinforce the point made in the previous chapter that 'reality' in the tourist-generating regions of the West is no less authentic than that in the more traditional societies in developing countries, which is itself no more authentic than the 'reality' of a resort geared to mass markets or a heavily visited 'art' city. Each is different; each may be pleasanter, safer, nastier or more fairly distributive of its wealth than the others, depending on the criteria against which it is measured; but all are constructs and thus potentially equally valid.

I say 'potentially' because there is obviously a problem if only one narrow group of interests is in control of the construction; even more so if that group comes from outside the area being constructed. Such a situation was exemplified by the case of 'Orientalism' (Said, 1978), which was imposed on the Middle East by British and French empire builders in the nineteenth century. Building on a fascination with the region's ancient past and on romantic perceptions of its people's primitiveness and sensuality, they created an image totally at odds with the way life was experienced there (and one which ignored post-pharaonic Arab prowess in the arts and sciences). Yet it is this image that has endured, thanks to the West's control over flows of information, and it has coloured the West's foreign policy towards the region, often to disastrous effect. Getting away from the propagation of 'false' images, of which tourists are sometimes the dupe, would require a new information order of the sort that was called for by the non-aligned countries in the 1970s. In other words it would require a much deeper structural change than could be effected at the level of the tourist.

Where tourism is concerned, perhaps it is time to seek an alternative to the term 'authenticity', for, while there is no doubt that tourism *has* changed the way some crafts and rituals are produced, the type of objects favoured and the meanings attached to them, this does not necessarily make them inauthentic. As Mathieson and Wall (1982: 171) have noted: 'one would not expect a vibrant art form to remain unchanged through centuries'. De Kadt (1979: 15) concurs: 'To be authentic, arts and crafts must be rooted both in historical tradition and in present day life; true authenticity cannot be achieved by conservation alone, since that leads to stultification.'

The *Alarde* ritual

Bearing this in mind, we shall now turn again to the *Alarde* of Fuenterrabia. Greenwood's (1977) study of this Basque ritual has become one of the most cited examples of the destructive and mercenary impacts of tourism on culture and heritage. His argument is that a ritual 'clearly not performed for outsiders ... *a performance for the participants*' (Greenwood, 1977: 133, original emphasis), commemorating a seventeenth-century victory over the French and uniting its people in the present, was turned into a show for tourists by the municipal government. This culminated in the declaration that it would be performed twice in the same day (which in fact appears not to have happened), causing consternation among participants and, in subsequent years, a marked loss of interest in performing the ritual: 'In the space of two years, what was a vital and exciting ritual had become an obligation to be avoided' (Greenwood, 1977: 135).

A close reading of Greenwood's study and of his 1989 epilogue to the second edition reveal something more complex, however. The ringing phrase 'Tourism killed the *Alarde*' has been cited with approval elsewhere (e.g. in Lanfant and Graburn, 1992: 102) but does not in fact appear in either edition. Rather, Greenwood states that, with the act of making the *Alarde* a public performance, 'a 350-year-old ritual died' (Greenwood, 1977: 136). Neither Greenwood nor any of those who quote his work acknowledge that it might have been the greed of the municipal government, rather than tourism *per se*, which did the 'killing', though obviously without tourism the authorities' greed might not have found expression. Also ignored is Greenwood's epilogue statement that the *Alarde* did not ultimately die but is 'imbued now with contemporary political significance as part of the contest over regional political rights in Spain' (Greenwood, 1989: 181). In other words it has changed and lost much of its earlier meaning, but has acquired a new meaning which is just as relevant to local participants. Greenwood goes on to acknowledge that tourism is not the only agent of change, that all cultures hold diversity and are continually changing, that 'some of what we see as destruction is construction; some is the result of the lack of any other viable options; and some the result of choices that could be made differently' (Greenwood, 1989: 182), and that characterizing all change as negative as part of an anthropological critique of modernization was at best a partial view of the process. (In other words, anthropologists had been imposing their own constructs of authenticity on 'traditional' societies.)

Greenwood admits in his epilogue that his earlier study 'was written as an expression of both anger and concern' (Greenwood, 1989: 181) and the earlier text is a largely first person account, full of expressions like 'I am terribly concerned', which suggest that the old *Alarde* had become special to him (a non-participant). I would further suggest that, like so many anthropologists who become possessive about the societies they study – and like 'travellers' who become upset when others discover 'their' secret cove, restaurant, craft seller – Greenwood had begun to think of the *Alarde* as 'my' ritual. This is a common and understandable reaction – and I would not deny that tourism did cause turmoil in the ritual, nor assert that change is universally good – but it is a phenomenon at least as interesting as that of tourism's impact on heritage.

Greenwood's 1977/89 studies can therefore be read as presenting a microcosm of the issues related to tourism's impact on heritage: adaptation to the pervasive influence of capitalism, the wielding of political power, conflict between groups whose interests may never be compatible, problems with alternatives, attitudes to the past and present, the construction of reality, and the appropriateness or otherwise of change. These are the questions that have to be considered when all tourism's impacts are examined. They must also lie behind any attempt to alter or 'reform' tourism, the subject of the final part of this book.

Part Three

What Is To Be Done?

9

Evaluating the evaluators

The previous chapters have demonstrated not only that the impacts of tourism are many, varied and far-reaching – a fact well charted by numerous researchers – but further that these effects are difficult to isolate, invariably inter-related and conditioned also by phenomena external to tourism, in particular the global political economy. While it is clear that tourism's impacts can be both positive and negative, depending in many cases on external circumstances, the number of writers opting to portray them in almost entirely negative terms has been steadily growing (see, for example, Britton, 1982; Wheeller, 1991; Cater, 1993; Burns and Holden, 1995; Pattullo, 1996). Such a development forms a necessary counterweight to the overoptimism of earlier studies that were concerned exclusively with economics, and to the fact that much research has been sponsored by the travel industry and understandably concentrates on favourable results and on maintaining growth.

How far, though, have critics of tourism taken account of the context in which it takes place? In investigating this it will obviously neither be possible nor desirable to examine everything that has been published. Instead we will look at a few key texts which can be considered as encompassing the major objections to tourism, or as representative of a prevailing stance towards it. The prescriptions or recommendations put forward by their authors will be discussed in terms of the extent to which these are desirable and realistic in the current organization of the global political economy.

This will be followed by a brief analysis of the concept of 'alternative' (also known as 'sustainable', 'responsible', etc.) tourism as the solution to the depredations of mass travel. The coherence of the concept and its potential to mitigate problems will be questioned, particularly in the light of people's motivation to travel. But first, let us turn to some individual works.

Some key works on tourism

Although it was written over twenty years ago, *The Golden Hordes* by Turner and Ash (1975) remains pertinent as the exemplar of early attempts to catalogue the evils of international tourism; many of its assertions are still repeated today. In particular, its depiction of a 'pleasure periphery' related to the core-periphery model of dependency theory has informed later work characterizing tourism as a form of imperialism. The authors do acknowledge that tourism takes place within a largely capitalist context of politics and economics and their detailed history of it from earliest times, together with references from film and literature, provide an entertaining read that confirms tourism as more than just a twentieth-century phenomenon.

However, within this context tourism is always viewed as a prime mover, always the cause and never an effect: 'The tourist is involved in nothing less than the rewriting of the economic and political geography of the world' (Turner and Ash, 1975: 251). The authors do not consider that tourism might be an expression of change in the international political economy rather than a driver of such change. Instead, they are carried away with their own polemic and are almost blind to any good that tourism can do, a fact which today must blunt their critique. It is, of course, easy to speak with the benefit of hindsight but it is notable that several of the outcomes of tourism feared by Turner and Ash have not come to pass. Venice, although in danger of becoming a tourism monoculture (van der Borg, Costa and Gotti, 1996), has nevertheless not become the Grand Hotels-backed theme park suggested by Turner and Ash on pages 138–9, while even their lower forecast of 1,300 million tourists roaming the globe annually by 2000 (p. 280) looks wildly inaccurate – fewer than half that number (594 million) were registered as arrivals in 1996 (WTO, 1997a) –

and again suggests a view of tourism as a driving force which ignores the way visitor numbers are affected by economic and political forces.

The Golden Hordes also cannot quite square its support for the Enlightenment view of cities as symbolic of progress and civilization – contrasted favourably with the current enthusiasm for nature and nostalgia – with its argument that decadent urban metropoles in the West are polluting the rest of the world with their tourists. Nor, even though it notes the congestion problems faced by many European cities, can it adequately explain the fact that the 'core' of Europe and North America receives far more visitors than the periphery.

Perhaps understandably, given their strong opposition to mass tourism, Turner and Ash do not make much attempt to offer solutions to the problems they identify. Those they do present emphasize the need for government control over the numbers of tourists to be allowed in, over taxation of tourists and over foreign ownership of land and businesses, but without suggesting how this control might be maintained in the face of global inequalities of power and a lack of economic alternatives. In sum – and like many who followed after them – Turner and Ash identify a number of serious problems resulting from tourism but do not suggest any more benign replacements for it as an economic activity.

The exertion of greater government control over tourism was also a priority for George Young (1973). Unlike many works, his critique, *Tourism: Blessing or Blight?*, concentrated largely on the UK and other developed countries, i.e. those with more chance of being able successfully to implement policies to control tourism. (It is ironic, therefore, that this apparent champion of public solutions should have gone on to be a member of the privatizing Thatcher government that turned out to be the most opposed to state intervention in the UK's recent history.)

Like Turner and Ash, Young provided a timely service by highlighting the hitherto glossed over social and environmental costs of tourism, thereby dispelling the idea that, at least economically, it was always a net provider of benefits. He was one of the first to catalogue the scale of the phenomenon and to point out the inadequacy of contemporary methods of quantification and forecasting – a problem which still exercises the WTO and other organizations (see Lickorish, 1997). His discussion of the conditions that predispose a person to travel (a certain level of education, income and free time) implicitly acknowledges the role of economic development in creating them, while his analysis of the industry's (lack of) structure and organization brings out the need for co-ordination between its various components and for a coherent overarching national tourism policy that also seeks to integrate the industry within national development.

Yet, despite asserting that the establishment of tourism must sometimes prevent the development of other industries, he does not really show which ones might be better, nor in what ways. Because he is principally concerned with berating the management of tourism in the UK, Young largely avoids consideration of the global forces it reflects. Certainly – and understandably for a future Conservative politician – he never questions the prevailing international economic order. Indeed, he sees the concentration of the tourism industry into a few mega-companies through vertical integration as a way of making it more efficient and coherent, rather than as the means of driving smaller, local businesses out of the market.

Young was nevertheless right in his prediction of greater industry consolidation and of the rise of computer reservation services and the use of information technology. His view that non-holiday-taking taxpayers and the government should not be supporting tourists via the subsidization of airports and tourist authorities is also beginning to be acted upon: airport tax is now a common addition to the price of an airline ticket and duty-free allowances are to be abolished within the EU from July 1999. However, the suggestion that a world tourist authority should be responsible for redirecting tourist flows away from overcrowded countries and towards those with 'spare capacity' appears unrealistic. Who would decide, using what criteria, when a resort was 'full up'? Who would be allowed to visit and who would be turned away? How would this be policed? In fact, this is an instance where 'the market' has worked fairly successfully, as tourists have voted with their feet when resorts have become unpleasantly overcrowded. Of course, this can mean physical and economic ruination for some resorts and their residents, but it can also act as a spur to improvements – as at Benidorm and Torbay – that bring the tourists back.

Young's insistence on planning and the need for a consistent tourism policy for the UK is laudable; integrating tourism within national economic policy makes sense for any country. The value of his critique lies in its thorough examination of one major tourism country's industry, rather than in any exploration beyond these boundaries.

A more global view was taken by Jost Krippendorf, who is probably also the author who has gone furthest in offering solutions for tourism's ills. *The Holiday Makers* (Krippendorf, 1987) was first published in German in 1984 and it introduces many German-language references that would previously have been unknown to Anglophone readers. (The continuing ignorance of each other's work among English-speaking researchers and those speaking other European languages remains a hindrance to a rounded appraisal of tourism.)

Although he provides convincing evidence of the social and environmental harm that can be done by tourism, and agrees with Young that local residents are often obliged by taxation to subsidize the holidays of their richer cousins, Krippendorf reserves much of his analysis for the tourists themselves. He also places them within a wider context. He sees the root of mass tourism in twentieth-century urban, industrialized everyday life, viewing it as a means of escape from the drudgery of work and therefore concluding that, if everyday life were more fulfilling, people would be happy to stay put, or at least to travel in a less destructive way (Krippendorf, 1987: 65–6). Young also made passing reference to this. Of the fact that 15 per cent of top earners in Britain did not take holidays, he noted: 'The homes of the very rich may be such that they have no reason to "escape" from them' (Young, 1973: 35).

There is undoubtedly some truth in this but it is not the whole truth. While it suggests that tourism is a response to political and economic forces, it ignores the role of other factors – climate, for instance, which, *pace* global warming, will never be as reliably or lengthily benign in some areas as it is in others. It treats tourists as a homogeneous group, capable of changing its habits and motivations *en masse*. Yet even mass travel is becoming more, not less, segmented. It also denies the possibility that there is a human imperative to travel which will be present whatever the circumstances in which we live, witness the growing enthusiasm for the possibility of public space travel (see Chapter 10).

Further, it does not explain why the vast majority do not seek a permanent holiday by dropping out of hated everyday society, but return after their two weeks away. (Some even use their holiday to reflect that home life is not so bad after all. A Russian conference delegate once told me a holiday to India had made her appreciate her own country more.) Of course, economic necessity makes it impossible for most of those dissatisfied with home life to become permanent tourists, but the paradox that, without the social changes and advances in productivity induced by industrialization, most people would not be able to go away in the first place, would have merited further investigation. What is it about capitalist development that both stimulates a desire to escape and provides the means to do it? Would socialist development have the same effect? Are societies from which the majority do not have the means of escape more content than the tourist-generating societies? These questions have not been asked; neither has there been much consideration of the way different classes are differently affected by urbanization – not all parts of any city are 'peopled by beings living in grey structures resembling silos and bunkers' (Krippendorf, 1987: 84). And while many residential areas do indeed lack recreational space or facilities, it is not correct to state, as Krippendorf (1987: 17) does, that 'cities have never been too concerned about the leisure and recreation needs of their inhabitants', since it is in these centres that one finds the most cinemas, theatres, galleries, swimmming pools, restaurants and nightclubs, etc.

Krippendorf discusses the symptoms of current economic and political organization as causes of mass tourism, without fully investigating what has produced these symptoms. His brief chapter on the economy is just a (valid) criticism of the philosophy of growth. The peculiar characteristics of capitalism and how this might make both economic activity and everyday life unalterable without itself being altered is not discussed and there is no attempt to link the economic to political considerations. This is all the more strange given that Krippendorf (1987: xx) does acknowledge that leisure and tourism 'are the results and at the same time integral parts of industrial society and its organization. Clearly then, leisure activities have an impact on the system and cannot be understood if they are isolated from their original determining factors'. However, he goes on to suggest that, once we have understood the connections and realized how the mechanism of tourism works, 'we can learn to control it, change it and improve it'. That this might not be possible on any great scale without fundamental system change does not seem to have been considered. Later Krippendorf (1987: 108) notes, seemingly realistically, that an ideal travel society 'will never exist, for its adversaries are too powerful. How can we overcome the almighty business-is-business principle or the unbridgeable North-South gap?' Yet he does not see this as a bar to a successful alteration of tourism. Certainly the effects of local, small-scale actions should not be underrated and may serve as a model for people elsewhere. However, the possibility of effecting major changes in the way tourism is conducted through such endeavours seems slight.

Pertinent prescriptions?

A similar disregard of the way tourism activity is a barometer of the global political economy is evident in the prescriptions offered in the final part of *The Holiday Makers*. They include:

■ The need to concentrate on people not profit in order to humanize tourism.

- The formulation of policies that ensure self-determination for all, while encouraging governments to impose restrictions where such self-determination would impinge on others or on the environment.
- The establishment of equal economic partnerships in the development of tourism, in which promoters and investors help finance basic infrastructure in the destination, the costs and benefits are spread between all parties and promoters, investors and hosts' representatives co-operate in planning, calculating costs and prices, organizing publicity and dividing up the profits.
- The redistribution of tourist flows, acknowledging the mass nature of tourism and accepting that special tourist enclaves can be a way of containing numbers.
- The need to prevent tourist destinations from becoming 'monocultures' and an insistence that locals be involved in their planning and running. In particular attempts should be made to keep land under local control through local government policies, while local culture and cuisine should be promoted over imports.
- Education. Industry personnel should receive a more thorough and comprehensive training, leading to a greater awareness of the destinations they promote; tourists should be encouraged to try new activities on holiday, to use the time to improve their personal relationships, to learn more about the countries they visit and to take a sensitive interest in their hosts; inhabitants of tourist destinations should be taught about the generating countries and behaviour *vis-à-vis* tourists discussed.
- An improvement in the everyday world of work and home. Unemployment would be fought through job shares, shorter hours, flexitime and flexi-careers, growth would be checked and the informal domestic economy would be boosted, with care of the sick and elderly, craft production, vegetable production and 'neighbourhood guidance' brought back to the home. The result would make the need for a holiday less desperate.

Few would disagree that, if implementable, these policies would ensure that hosts received more benefit from and paid fewer costs for tourism development, while guests would have a more fulfilling experience. Yet, despite one or two concrete suggestions such as showing incoming airline passengers a film of their destination, requiring components of the tourism industry to draw up a code of practice and providing a list of regional planning measures purporting to obviate mistakes in construction at holiday resorts, in most cases no explanation is given of how these prescriptions would be enforced. More importantly, it is not clear how some parties could be persuaded to accept a drop in income or influence, especially given the short-term nature of much business planning.

As Krippendorf himself admits ('to my knowledge there are very few examples of such co-operation' [Krippendorf, 1987: 114]), most tourism businesses are not altruistic and many, especially the smaller concerns, work to tight margins. In a global economy in which not to make a profit is to go under, any talk of spreading costs or limiting numbers is unlikely to be well received. Keeping control in local hands is more easily said than done: in disadvantaged regions locals might prefer to sell their land for needed short-term gain, the exploitation of its sudden commercial value being the only way to play a system they are not powerful enough to beat. And, of course, local elites are just as capable of keeping control for their own ends as any tour operator. Indeed the question of who should represent the local community – private business people? residents of non-tourism areas? job-seekers? public authorities? – is not addressed. Yet self-interest is not the monopoly of the tourism industry – conflicts over control and direction are replicated within all communities, whether local, national or international, and it is a mistake to assume that governments can always further the interests of all their citizens. That is why, when given the opportunity to do so, people support different political parties.

Finally, while some tourists do want to learn new things on holiday, many do not and would find attempts to encourage such self-development bewildering or patronizing. Krippendorf does tackle this point by emphasizing that a more 'humanized' society might make holidays less necessary but, again, he gives no indication of how a less growth-orientated economy would be brought about. If the 'too powerful adversaries' are never confronted, success is only ever going to be achieved at the margins.

More detailed and less Utopian recommendations are laid down by de Kadt (1979: 339–44). Drawn up following a seminar on how to take account of tourism's social and cultural impacts when making decisions on its development, they are aimed principally at governments and planners in developing countries, rather than at tourists and outside investors as well. To an extent, then, since fewer parties are involved, the recommendations should be easier to implement. The advice they contain seems sound:

- Plan tourism as part of the national development effort and integrate it with other sectors, as well as with the planning of additional infrastructure and services for the existing local population and any job-related influx of people.

- Carry out impact studies before approving tourism projects and establish maximum acceptable rates of tourism growth and hotel construction.
- Capitalize on the country's unique features to reduce competition, maximize local resources and help poorer, rural sections of society to supply food and craftware through co-operatives and credit schemes, etc. as well as encouraging small-scale entrepreneurship via training courses and technical assistance.
- Pay close attention to the terms on which transnational companies manage tourism firms in destination countries.
- Actively consult host populations and ensure co-ordination between all agencies (ministries of housing, employment, environment, culture) with an interest in tourism.
- Seek markets with different seasonal patterns and encourage tourists from a variety of social and regional origins.
- Co-ordinate regional marketing and development efforts where many small countries compete to ensure that all may profit.
- Avoid always ploughing profits or budget surpluses back into tourism investment.

The question that is avoided in all of this is why powerful transnational industry groups should see a more co-operative approach to tourism development as in their interest and how they could be persuaded to endorse such recommendations. A country that was freely able to follow these guidelines would almost certainly achieve a profitable tourism industry that enhanced national development with minimum disruption to indigenous lifestyles. But how many countries, developing or otherwise, have done so? Examples of actions taken in pursuance of any of the suggestions cited above are rare. True, some airlines now show films about their passengers' destination on board (though how many passengers are watching is another matter); the Tourism Industry Association of Canada has produced a code of ethics for the industry as well as guidelines for tour operators and hotels (D'Amour, 1992); and individual tourism projects in developing countries have been successfully created using local resources and personnel (Saglio, 1979). On the other hand, Turkey, a relatively recent entrant into the tourism business, has permitted uncontrolled building by outside interests along parts of its coastline and has done little to discourage pollution of resources; the food prepared for tourists on most Caribbean islands is still imported, not sourced from local producers; and significant numbers of surveyed tourists still profess no interest in what goes on outside their hotel. Without addressing the framework conditions that have have shaped such behaviour, there can be little chance of success.

The 'alternative' alternative

It would be wrong to argue that the proposed solutions discussed above have had no impact. For beyond raising general awareness, they have been incorporated as the tenets of what has become known as alternative tourism, a concept which, in academic circles and much of the media, has become the new orthodoxy. In addition it has been espoused by a number of pressure groups, including the Ecumenical Council on Third World Tourism, Tourism Concern and the Centre for the Advancement of Responsive Tourism. Since 1993 there has been a journal – the *Journal of Sustainable Tourism* – dedicated to research in this field.

The term 'alternative tourism' first seems to have been coined in the early 1980s (Lanfant and Graburn, 1992). It is probably the most used of the interchangeable terms 'responsible', 'appropriate', 'green' and 'soft' tourism, although 'sustainable tourism' – a borrowing from the environmental movement – has gained ground recently. In keeping with the number of names for it, there is no single agreed definition, but it is generally understood to refer to tourism that is small scale, geared to individual travellers, organized by independent operators but controlled by the host community, environmentally sustainable and culturally enhancing. Such characteristics will, it is thought, cause tourism to be sustainable since hosts will benefit, carrying capacity limits will not be exceeded and tourists will continue to visit thanks to the ongoing 'unspoiltness' of the destination.

Again, few could argue with the apparent logic behind this, but the number of such ideal destinations or operations remains dwarfed by the mass-market norm, while the cases in which advocates of alternative tourism have been able to alter harmful practices have been few. Tourism Concern contributed to getting UK law changed so that paedophiles on sex tours arrested for offences abroad can be prosecuted in UK courts, instead of simply being deported and then allowed to go free. Its campaign over the use of slave labour to build a tourism infrastructure for 'visit Myanmar (Burma)' year in 1996 also seems to have dissuaded some people from travelling to the country – occupancy rates in most hotels built at the time are at around 15 per cent (*Guardian*, 22 December 1997). However, Burma is hardly a major destination and child-sex tourism is a small-scale activity in terms of numbers. In general, and like the authors discussed above, the proponents of alternative tourism have been better at highlighting the negative side of tourism than at providing cures.

There are several reasons for this. One is the by now familiar failure to analyse tourism within a wider framework. If, as Hunter (1997) has shown, sustainable tourism researchers have largely ignored the wider debate over the meaning of sustainable development and viewed sustainable/alternative tourism as a means in itself rather than a contribution to sustainable development, we should not be surprised at their neglect of other broader contexts. Yet, if the Burmese military regime has been using slave labour to build tourism facilities, we can be sure that it has been using it in all sorts of other areas too. Perversely, perhaps tourism has helped bring the long-standing loathsomeness of the Burmese regime to world attention by providing an example of its disregard for human rights. Changing its behaviour would depend on understanding the forces that might make it act as it does. Similarly we need to know what rationale might impel companies to operate in such a country. Is it malice? Greed? A misguided notion of bringing work and income to the Burmese people? Or the belief that competition elsewhere is too intense for the company to make enough to pay its employees a decent wage? Such questions have not been sufficiently addressed.

Second, as Wheeller (1991) has persuasively argued, by its very nature alternative tourism cannot deal with the volume of people currently travelling. Indeed, it actually fuels that volume by encouraging people to go to previously unvisited places and has been used by the more shrewd tour operators as a marketing/growth tool to appeal to 'premium rate' tourists, either by opening up new areas or by extending the season, a point not lost on Krippendorf (1987: 38). Alternative tourism then, 'while claiming to be the "good tourism" has not, in spite of its forceful declared opposition, broken radically with the "other tourism" (Lanfant and Graburn, 1992: 112). On the contrary, just as 'low-impact' backpackers have popularized destinations that are now mainstream (Pryer, 1997), alternative tourism is more likely to be a precursor of mass tourism and a contributor to the pioneering stage of Butler's (1980) tourist area lifecycle model.

Further criticisms have been made – small-scale tourism cannot always provide a viable level of income and employment; educating the tourist is a very long-term process the financing and logistics of which have not been addressed – but the most persistent of these is that the notion of alternative tourism is elitist. By emphasizing individual over mass travel, nature- or culture-based holidays over beach and nightlife vacations and high pricing over discounting, it appeals and is available only to a small section of tourists, disregarding those who may be in most need of a holiday. In other words, as well as ignoring the forces that have shaped current tourism practices, alternative tourism also omits consideration of the varied reasons why different people travel. It is to this that we shall now turn in our next chapter.

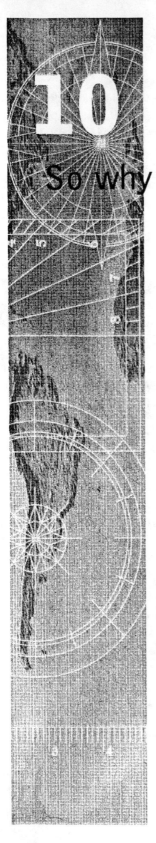

10

So why do people travel?

Travel is motivated by 'going *away* from' rather than 'going towards' something or somebody.

(Krippendorf, 1987: 29)

We travel long roads and cross the water to see what we disregard when it is under our eyes.

(Pliny the Younger)

These two statements, separated by almost 2,000 years, demonstrate two ways of looking at travel. One sees it as a response to conditions at home, with the final destination of little importance. The other views it as motivated by the lure of the new and the different. Pliny's letter goes on to note that many people are more familiar with the attractions of distant places than with those of their home, an observation that is as true today as it was then. This chapter will suggest that both contentions are valid, but that they are indispensable to one another. For it will argue that the need to escape from 'ordinary' life is not just a product of the twentieth century and that, while types and means of tourism are historically and culturally determined, the urge to travel is not. In other words, this chapter will argue that it is the combination of the opportunity to travel, greatly expanded during the twentieth century, with the innate desire to explore and seek new experiences which has created the unstoppable juggernaut of tourism. It will then discuss the wholly unremarkable – yet often ignored – proposition that people engage in tourism because they enjoy it (c.f. drugs) and will suggest that tourism has given more people more happiness than almost anything else. In exploring the importance of tourism to tourists, particular attention will be paid to the post-1989 experiences of Eastern Europeans, as political restrictions on travel were lifted.

The emphasis of this book has been on the need to take account of the context in which tourism takes place, with the suggestion that it acts as a barometer of the global political economy rather than a driver of it. The idea that tourism is a response to a need to escape from the division of labour arising from the present political economy would clearly fit in with this. Certainly the need may have been made more acute by the present-day demands of work, by the perception that society has become dehumanized through reliance on machines, by the pace of change, etc. However, the desire to escape everyday life long predates industrialization and is common to most cultures – even if it has been realized in different ways.

The function of escape

Indeed, it may be more helpful to think of 'escape' as a natural human instinct, a way of maintaining a balanced society through the temporary departure from everyday life, or what Jafari (1987) has called 'the ordinary', and achieved by a variety of means, not all of them spatial. Hence the existence of religious festivals – many of them an excuse for a party – such as the Roman Saturnalia, Celtic and Scandinavian pre-Christian solstice celebrations, Hindu Diwali, and Buddhist water festivals, as well as Christmas and Easter. Hence also the use of hallucinogenic drugs in many cultures to transport selected members mentally away from normal life, as well as the use of art and music to focus the mind on things distinct from the workaday world. Travel was significant as well, of course; it was a favourite method for Victorian ladies of sufficient income to find release from rigid social expectations or to do something for themselves following years of caring for ailing parents. But it was available only to the few, while festivals were all-inclusive and even some forms of art, notably that embodied in the great churches, could be experienced by everyone.

Looked at in this way, escape can be considered a normal part of human existence, a temporary alteration that ensures the smooth functioning of society or, to borrow a phrase of Krippendorf's (1987: xv), 'the valve that maintains the world in good running order', a need that is unlikely to disappear, whatever the type of society. The question then becomes, why is tourism now the preferred means of escape. The answer lies partly, as suggested above, in the technological advances and productivity increases discussed in previous chapters that have put tourism within reach of a majority of the population of the industrialized countries. It is also related to the fact that organized religion is on the decline in the West and that hallucinogenic drugs are illegal (though still used) in most societies. But I suggest it revolves around the fact that the urge to travel is inborn.

Historical precedents

Humans have been on the move since they learned to walk upright. Initially, such movement – in the form of migrations, hunting trips and warfare – was about survival but, at least since recorded histroy began, curiosity has also been an element. We now know that the Vikings and the Irish both ventured across the Atlantic and beat Columbus to America. The Romans were searching for the Hyperboreans when they came across the British Isles. Not content with pushing beyond the boundaries of the Persian empire, Alexander the Great was preparing to sail around Arabia when he died. The urge to discover what lies over the horizon has always been a constant – and not just among Europeans. The Arabs and Chinese were both long-haul sea voyagers. Moreover, the latter, who sailed the South Seas and the Indian Ocean, did not espouse the aggressively commercial habits of the Portuguese who followed them, but were more interested in diplomatic and governmental objectives (Finney, 1985a: 201). But perhaps the greatest travellers were the Polynesians.

Polynesian peoples who lived along the shores of south-east Asia began to spread eastwards into the Pacific using their canoes some 5,000 years ago. Around 3,500 years ago they reached and colonized the archipelagos of Fiji, Tonga and Samoa (Finney, 1985b), a voyage of some 2,000 miles from their base. Here they remained for several centuries, but eventually they set off again and had reached the Marquesas Islands in the middle of the Pacific by the middle of the first century BC. Thence they sailed north, south-east and south-west over seemingly never ending seas to reach Hawaii, Easter Island and New Zealand. They may even have made a round trip to South America (they are known to have had the sweet potato, which originated in South America) (Finney, 1985b: 171). Various factors have been put forward as explanations for the Polynesians' extraordinary voyages. Population pressure is one. The inheritance system of Polynesian society, in which the oldest son gained everything, leaving younger brothers without lands of their own, is another. But these cannot wholly explain why their settlers largely ignored the huge island of Borneo, which was much nearer to their starting point, nor why, once they had started, they just kept on going, at a rate that cannot be accounted for by carrying capacity overload in their new colonies: 'these seafarers seem to have become intoxicated with the discovery of new lands, with using a voyaging technology they alone possessed to sail where no one had ever been before' (Finney, 1985b: 169).

It is hard not to see an element of curiosity in this. The point is not that the Polynesians should be thought of as tourists, that would be absurd. But their instincts in moving ever outward do suggest an innate interest in travel that would make it very hard to deter. Indeed, a similar urge can be detected today in the realm of spaceflight, which Pyne (1988) has likened to the great ages of discovery in Europe, and in the growing enthusiasm for space tourism.

The new space race

Human curiosity about the stars is probably not much younger than the urge to wander, though interest in visiting them did not really begin until the nineteenth century, when Jules Verne's stories caught the imagination and technological advance started to make it look a possibility. Until the 1990s the space age was driven by state-centred political and military concerns, notably the Cold War, but economic imperatives are now growing in importance with the proliferation of commercial communications satellite systems and the expectation that other technologies, e.g. remote sensing, will become profitable in the medium term. Throughout the period, however, there has been a persistent lobby (strongest in the USA but active elsewhere) pushing for opportunities for the public to fly in space, with the eventual aim of colonizing the solar system.

It must be acknowledged that many such lobbyists share an imperialist-type mentality that is at least as interested in exploitation as it is in exploration, and do not see the irony that they may be leaving a planet scarred by their activities only to go and repeat their despoliation somewhere else. Nevertheless, the response to advertisements in the USA and UK for civilians to fly on the *Challenger* Space Shuttle and take part in the British Juno mission on the Russian orbital laboratory *Mir* was enormous and not confined to 'space cadets'. The American choice, Christa McAuliffe, was a teacher, the UK's Helen Sharman a very down-to-earth food technologist. In 1985 Society

Expeditions, which already organized tours to the Antarctic, launched Project Space Voyage with the goal of operating passenger flights by the mid-1990s. Two years later they had received 10,000 enquiries from over forty countries and had taken about 250 deposits – at $52,000 each – from people ready to sign up for a place in space in an as yet unbuilt vehicle. These were returned when the requisite vehicle failed to materialize (the technical challenges are enormous). However, other tour operators in the USA are taking bookings today and a $10 million prize competition to build a spacecraft capable of taking three people twice into suborbital space, 100 kms above the Earth, is now under way.

Personally, I think that, because of the technical difficulties, space tourism is much further away than its supporters pretend. For our purposes, however, what matters is the interest shown and there is no doubting it. Such interest could be dismissed as the ultimate in one-upmanship, espoused by the rich for its status value only, were it not for the fact that many of its keenest fans are young engineers of relatively modest means. Moreover, spaceflight is dangerous, uncomfortable, has periods of extreme tedium and can be literally nauseating – which means, incidentally, that it fulfils many of Boorstin's (1964) criteria for travel as opposed to tourism. And, while the cost of a putative spaceflight is currently prohibitive, ordinary people are visiting space vicariously in their droves, via such television and film series as the various *Star Treks*, through visits to launch sites and trips to the Air and Space Museum in Washington, which alone receives 8 million visitors annually. (On a more lighthearted note, we might also recall that the first outing for the Oscar-winning plasticene creations Wallace and Gromit was a day out to the Moon.)

Motivation

So the human urge for change, for seeing over the next horizon, has been a constant throughout history and present in many varied societies. And if we turn to the commonest reasons tourists themselves give when questioned about why they take a holiday (see Table 10.1), we find phrases like 'to see different places and things', 'to broaden one's education', 'for excitement and adventure'. We also see more prosaic answers, such as 'to get away from bad weather', 'to eat good food' and 'to have time for family and friends'. These answers have been associated with the satisfaction of a variety of needs, ranging from ensuring basic physical well-being to achieving a heightened sense of oneness with others or with 'something higher' (see Table 10.2). Although tourists may not consciously recognize such needs, it is easy to see

Table 10.1   Ten reasons for taking a holiday commonly cited by tourists

To have time for family and friends
To be with others and have fun
For rest and relaxation
To discover new places and things/experience a different culture
To experience nature
To broaden one's education (through museum visits, etc.)
To get away from bad weather
To eat good food
For excitement and adventure
To visit places one has heard about/see famous attractions

Sources: Young, 1973; Krippendorf, 1987; Poon, 1993; Ryan, 1997.

Table 10.2   A summary of motivations for tourism

Intrinsic factors

Physical needs	for bodily and mental refreshment; to improve one's health; to master a sport or to take part in exciting activities such as theme park rides or whitewater rafting
Cultural needs	for knowledge of other people and places; to see art, architecture, customs; to attend specific events, e.g. the Bayreuth Ring Cycle
(Inter)personal needs	to visit friends and relatives; to make new friendships or cement old ones; to seek new experiences and have a change from one's permanent environment
Status and prestige needs	to further one's education, pursue hobbies or business; to be seen in the most fashionable or exclusive places and to return home with the tan, photos and souvenirs to prove it
Spiritual needs	to find something higher than oneself, either through a feeling of heightened solidarity with other holidaymakers, through experience of a culture deemed more 'authentic' or through visiting a site considered meaningful or sacred

Extrinsic factors

Economic	income levels, nature of work and holiday entitlements
Social	level of education; class membership; influence of family, peer groups and the culture of one's society
Political	government restrictions on travel abroad
Physical	age; sex; mobility; existence of travel-facilitating infrastructure and technology

how they can be translated into different types of holiday activity. And it is also easy to see how they have been derived from more general work in psychology on the motivations that drive all human activity (see, for example, Maslow, 1943).

Holiday choices are also affected by other extrinsic factors such as income, education, peer group preferences and culture (Table 10.2) and even by geographical factors like contiguity with other states, distance from major destination countries, etc. The oft-quoted statistic that only around 10 per cent of Americans own a passport conceals the fact that vast numbers of them take part in domestic tourism, as might be expected of a huge country that is far from the world's top destination region (Europe), has a continental economy and a history of relative isolationism. Obviously it is not necessary to go abroad to travel; indeed, in terms of numbers, domestic tourism is a much larger phenomenon than its international sibling. And the reasons for choosing a holiday presented in Table 10.1 apply just as much as to travel abroad.

Most tourists cite a combination of reasons for choosing a particular holiday but, of course, not each of them is equally important to everyone. Package tourists spend 80 per cent of their time in the environs of their hotel and, even though sitting round a pool differs from what they do at home, are therefore unlikely to be broadening their education. People's needs also change over their lifecycle, the young independent traveller eventually giving way to the ageing tourist who just wants a rest, for example, or they may take a main holiday to satisfy one set of needs and several short breaks to satisfy others. It would be wrong to pretend that all tourists are engaged in a Pliny-like voyage of discovery. But it does seem as if tourism, in its variety and its ability to satisfy quite diverse needs, now offers the most convenient and accessible means of escape from the ordinary. And it is surely right to suggest that, whatever the holiday type, all tourists are bent on enjoying themselves. By and large, they succeed in doing so.

The fun element

We are no doubt all familiar with horror stories of people's nightmare holidays, involving delayed flights, unbuilt hotels, all-night noise, terrible food, accidents, illness and crime. But the fact that they make the news suggests they are the exception which proves the rule that tourism is one of the most enjoyable aspects of life. Indeed, 95 per cent of UK doctors recommend holidays as an alternative to medication – especially for stress-related complaints – while Australian researchers found that most people experience a lessening of tension and fatigue after the first four or five days of a holiday

(Norfolk, 1994). That the benefits of a holiday may be substantial yet unavailable to those most in need of them – e.g. the elderly, the disabled, the poor and the unemployed – has been recognized and acted upon in a few countries, notably Switzerland, which provide social funds that subsidize or otherwise facilitate holidays for the disadvantaged (Teuscher, 1983; Hughes, 1991). In such cases, holidays are accepted 'as an investment in the well-being and social fabric of the country' (Hughes, 1991: 196).

The East European example

The importance of tourism to the well-being of citizens and to their economically productive capacities (Hall, 1991: 84) was also recognized in the Eastern bloc where, at least until the fall of Communism, social tourism was most developed. In fact, it was the predominating mode, with most holidays being of a group nature and organized by trade unions, schools and other institutions with the state covering most of the costs of accommodation and transport (Hall, 1991: 84). A far wider range of society than in the West was thus enabled to go on holiday but their choice of destination was much more limited. For ideological and political reasons few citizens were allowed to leave the Eastern bloc: for them tourism meant either domestic or intra-bloc holidays.

All this changed when the Berlin Wall came down and Eastern bloc citizens became free to travel further afield. Between 1987 and 1991 Bulgaria and Poland registered an almost 300 per cent increase in travel abroad, Czechoslovakia 428 per cent, the Soviet Union 214 per cent and Romania a huge 790 per cent (Hall, 1995: 229, table 13.4). Hungary and Yugoslavia with 'only' a 99 per cent and 80 per cent increase respectively (Hall, 1995: 229, Table 13.4) had long had more liberal travel regimes. Most major West European countries experienced a 20–60 per cent rise in arrivals from Central and Eastern Europe between 1989 and 1991, while Turkey posted a 165 per cent increase (Hall, 1995: 231). In 1994 the Czech airline's (CSA) most popular non-European destination was Thailand (Hall, 1995: 236).

We should not place too much reliance on these figures. For one thing they do not differentiate between 'true' holidaymakers and excursionists, cross-border petty traders or migrant labour, while CSA is popular among non-nationals as a relatively cheap airline (Hall, 1995: 236). But if we bear in mind that unfavourable exchange rates during the period (and the collapse of much social tourism organization) will have prevented many people from travelling, the figures do look impressive and follow the pattern estalished in South Korea when travel restrictions were abolished there. This is especially true when we consider that the region's own tourism 'product' is excellent and diverse. From Black Sea beaches to the Tatra Mountains (complete with ski resorts), to forests, lakes and the Danube Delta, to a highly developed historical and cultural legacy, not to mention the best mineral spa facilties in the world, Eastern Europeans have been able to enjoy world-class attractions on their doorstep. Yet, since it became possible, they have shown a marked predilection for travel elsewhere.

Clearly, there can be no single reason for this: the possibility of visiting friends and relatives on the other side of the Iron Curtain, the lure of Western markets – in which both to buy and sell – and, doubtless, the desire to experience those countries so derided by the socialist governments will all have played a role. But it seems not unreasonable to assume that, just as a holiday has come to be regarded as a necessity in the UK (Hughes, 1991: 194), so Eastern bloc citizens viewed the freedom of travel that existed elsewhere as an essential component of normal life, as it became after their governments signed the Helsinki Agreement on Human Rights: 'in 1989 [tourism] is partly responsible for bringing down some of the boundaries between East and West, as those in Eastern Europe have demanded the right to travel and to gaze upon those in the west' (Urry, 1990: 156). In other words, tourism has become for Eastern Europeans both a means of enhancing their well-being through escape from everyday life and a way of satisfying their curiosity about unknown lands and people and they will be loath to see any new restrictions placed upon it.

It is this bringing together in tourism of the twin possibilities of escaping from the ordinary and investigating other places that has made it so popular. Whether tourism is a search for perceived 'authenticity', or whether it is truer to say that 'many tourists, perhaps even most, seek not authenticity but merely diversion in their travels – sun, sand, sea, and sex' (Goodale and Godbey, 1988: 214) is largely irrelevant – if we interpret authenticity as 'something higher than ourselves' tourism can potentially satisfy both aspirations, and others. Now that travel is so accessible, at least to populations in the West (and increasingly to those in the East), the likelihood that people will stop wanting to become tourists looks slim indeed.

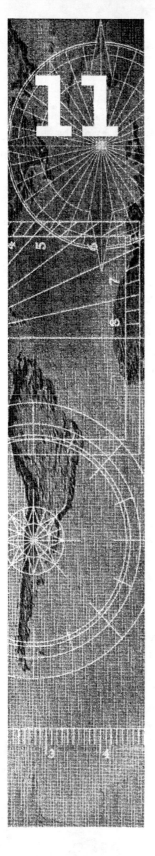

Conclusion

It is probably impossible, and certainly meaningless, to make a yes or no pronouncement on
whether tourism today is a good or bad thing,
since every situation in which it occurs is
different. More importantly, the feelings of those
involved in or affected by it also vary markedly.
Tourism provides needed employment and
income – often not of the most lucrative or
satisfying kind, but equally often of the only kind
available. Tourism has enhanced some environments and degraded others. It has been one
among many agents of negative and positive
change – as perceived by different groups. In
short, it is a complex and contradictory phenomenon that needs to be looked at from a variety of
angles but which above all should not be seen in
a vacuum.

Context and contradictions

This book has attempted to show that the impacts
of tourism cannot be divorced from the wider
context in which it occurs, a fact which has at last
begun to be acknowledged (see, for example,
Hall, 1994; Wall, 1996). While tourism itself has
shaped the economies of many countries and the
everyday life of their people, the phenomenon

has also been conditioned by the political and economic organization of what is now a global system, and by the attitudes and social relations that result from this organization. Tourism is only one of many causes of change. Not only may it not be the most important, it may be impossible to separate from the others, and it needs to be considered as part of an interwoven tapestry of agents of change.

It has been evident in the chapters covering its environmental, economic and social effects that tourism can be both a blight and a blessing, depending on the circumstances in which it is introduced and the way it is developed. Furthermore, tourism may not only be a blight in some destinations and a blessing in others, it may, within the same destination, be a blight for some yet a blessing for others, depending on who is affected and how. This is why researchers have often produced what Wall (1996: 208) calls 'contradictory findings', showing, for example, that tourism destroys culture on the one hand and preserves or revives it on the other. Each finding may be correct for the situation studied. In addition, at least some of the impacts identified by outside researchers as 'negative', such as changes in social structures or traditions, are often welcomed by the resident population (c.f. Wall, 1996: 207–8). Just as early studies of tourism and those carried out under the aegis of the industry emphasized the economic benefits of tourism to the exclusion of other, often negative aspects, so at least some current research seems to be based on the researchers' own (usually Western biased) perceptions of what is best for people, without attempting to consult them. Similarly, the largely beneficial impact on tourists themselves is often left out of the equation altogether. Clearly, if the benefits to tourists are achieved at the expense – economic, environmental or social – of others, as is sometimes the case, especially where international flows from the developed to the developing world occur, this is unjust. But the positive impact of tourism on tourists should not be forgotten.

Finally, while it would be wrong to attempt to balance any harm done to residents with the good done to tourists, in general terms a negative impact in one area (e.g. the environment) can be offset by a positive impact in another (e.g. the economy) and vice versa. In other words, just as the impacts of tourism cannot be isolated from other sources of change, so the different types of tourism impacts – environmental, economic, social, cultural – cannot be separated from each other but combine to produce a totality of 'tourism effects', some of which will have to be traded off against each other in order to arrive at a balanced assessment of whether tourism is a worthwhile undertaking for a particular community or destination. It is only by taking this more holistic view, which, as was discussed in Chapter

2, has largely been ignored as a method of academic research, that we can hope to further the progress that has been made in understanding tourism processes.

Conflicts of interest

'Holism' should not imply studying only the whole to the total exclusion of any consideration of the parts, however (McLean, 1981). Rather, both should be examined in order to gain the fullest picture of any phenomenon. After all, tourism has never been a monolith – and is even less of one today thanks to the proliferation of flexible packages, independent travel and niche holidays – and tourists are not a homogeneous group. The same goes for host communities themselves, which are comprised of people with a variety of different interests: in business, in employment, in bringing up children, in having sports facilities and a nightlife, in peace and quiet. Some of these will overlap, of course, but we must also acknowledge that 'conflicts of values may be an intrinsic, irremovable element in human life' (Berlin, 1997: 238). It is therefore essential, as Wall (1996: 208) points out, to investigate how types of tourism, community characteristics and the nature of host–guest interactions affect the impacts created. But at the same time, we must look at the overall international context in which these types of tourism are implemented, and these different communities grow up. This means analysing the external political and economic forces that shape tourism activity. It also means taking account of the effects of other industries (shaped by those same forces) on economies, environments and people.

For other industries also have good and bad impacts, depending on the context and way in which they are developed, which also have to be traded off against each other if we are to understand their overall positive or negative balance, and which must be weighed against those of tourism when alternatives to it are considered. It is wrong to see tourism as uniquely bad – the impression gained from much literature and talk at conferences – *all* industries create impacts. As was highlighted in Chapter 5, we have only to think of the pollution caused by so much heavy industry, not to mention the social consequences when villages are forcibly resettled to make way for industrial production (as with the oil industry in Nigeria, for instance) or those arising from the removal of green recreational spaces to make way for factories in many European countries. The impacts of manufacturing industries are not the same as those of service industries and, of course, on balance the changes they produce may be considered worthwhile because of the other benefits (e.g. employment) they provide, but it is only by taking all this into account that we will form a true picture of the benefits and costs of tourism.

Moreover, other industries are also influenced by the sorts of issues that have emerged from previous chapters: many of the factors that help determine whether tourism will have a postive or negative effect on a community overall can also be applied to other sectors. They include:

- The question of control over land-use and land speculation. The latter is a chief cause of inflation and of the pricing of land and housing out of the reach of local people.
- The question of who controls both the long-term development of the industry and the day-to-day running of it in any given destination, the general expectation being that keeping control in the hands of the – often undefined – local community will be more beneficial for local residents.
- The question of alternatives. Is tourism to be a 'monoculture', making a destination or country riskily overreliant on a sole source of income, or merely one of a number of industries?
- The question of how far tourism is integrated into a country or region's national development plan or overall economy.

Relying on any industry as a sole source of revenue is dangerous – witness the widespread job losses and impoverishment in Zambia following the collapse of copper prices in the 1970s, or the desolation of the UK steel town of Consett after British Steel closed down its works. And the effect of other industries in areas where local people have no say in local development can be just as devastating as that of tourism. One thinks again of the fate of the Ogoni people of Nigeria, or the forcible resettlement of whole villages in China, Malaysia and India to make way for hydroelectric dams. Again, some of these issues may be more applicable to tourism than to other industries and vice versa. Where land prices are concerned, house prices often fall when a factory is built in their vicinity and a manufacturing complex, once built, can often increase output without encroaching on further land. But the general point that all industries are affected by their external contexts is still valid.

If we can identify the areas likely to affect the equitability of tourism (and other) development, it is also possible theoretically to suggest measures to help make a more balanced development possible (c.f. de Kadt, 1979; Mathiesen and Wall, 1982: 177–80; Krippendorf, 1987). Some of these were discussed in Chapter 9 and we will reiterate them only briefly here. They include the need for adequate forecasting in order to predict future congestion; the need for integrated, long-term planning and impact assessment that avoids the temptation to go for short-term gain; the need to set proper goals and identify which areas should be the main beneficiaries of tourism; the need to involve local people in the decision-making process and the industry itself; and the need for local authority control of land-use. These remain the sorts of solutions put forward in many case studies (see, for example, Akama, 1997).

However, as was also discussed in Chapter 9, such solutions are often very difficult to implement, simply because they too cannot be carried out in isolation. Because of the plurality of interests in present-day society, a gain for some is almost inevitably going to be a loss for others and, even where they are willing to put their ordinary citizens first (by no means a foregone conclusion), national and local governments are constrained by the international context. For instance, while tourism's development as a monoculture can be the result of poor planning, it can also occur because no economic alternatives are available thanks to the way the world economy is organized. If this is not taken into account, if we do not 'deal with "the obvious", but critical fact that tourism needs to be situated in capitalist society' (Hall, 1994: 192) no large-scale alteration in the way tourism is developed is likely to be either conceivable or practical.

Tourism as both driven and driving

Just as tourism's impacts must be considered within a wider context, so the whole phenomenon of present-day international tourism must be viewed as conditioned (but not caused) by the major features of (postindustrial) late capitalist world society: globalization and interdependence; the dominance of Western attitudes to nature and to the past, with a mistrust of the concept of linear progress; and the breakdown of formerly discrete spheres of activity such as work and leisure, with the emphasis on a plurality of views, on cultural relativism and on the importance of image and spectacle (Urry, 1990).

Thus tourism acts both as a barometer of the international system and a means by which it is perpetuated. As we saw in Chapter 3, tourism flourishes best in stable, peaceful economies and can be severely affected by political or economic change, while the international institutions of tourism reflect both the existence of prevailing power blocs and the imperative of profit. Wider attitudes to nature and culture are highlighted by the current interest in environmental and heritage tourism (Chapter 8), while the involvement of some tourists in socially damaging activities such as prostitution acts to magnify pre-existing situations. At the same time, tourism itself helps to spread the features it is reflecting. This is perhaps best illustrated with the example of tourism's role in the economic restructuring of the Central and Eastern European countries as they become incorporated into the world system.

Hall (1991: 11–12) has noted six ways that tourism aids this process: as a means of supplying hard currency and ameliorating balance of payments problems; as a catalyst for social change through the exposure of host populations to the outside world via tourists; as a symbol of freedom embodied in the new found possibilities to travel to the West (or elsewhere); as a means of improving local infrastructures through the upgrading of facilities; as an integral component of the transition to a market economy; and as a facet of commercial development through the growth of business tourism. Of course, other industries also bring in foreign currency, have an effect on infrastructures and are part of the privatization and decentralization process integral to a market economy, while the media are just as influential in bringing about social change and freedom can equally well be symbolized by access to a telephone network, the abolition of censorship and the availability of a choice of foreign and domestic consumer goods. However, tourism may be unique in having a role to play in all these categories – not because it is an autonomous driver of change but because it so well reflects all the major facets of twentieth-century society.

Theoretically, then, the study of tourism can be used to highlight trends in and workings of the international political economy and can be conceptualized as a reflection of changing social attitudes which are themselves shaped by external developments. By examining the varying effects of different types (parts) of tourism on different types of communities, as well as looking at the whole, and at the external forces that in turn interact with this whole, we may be able to create a more holistic, integrated study of tourism.

The question of capitalism

At the practical level, it has been argued throughout this book that tourism cannot be fundamentally altered so that its costs and benefits are more equally shared without reform of the capitalist system. The question that then would have to be considered is how far capitalism is susceptible to change (and whether any new system would ultimately turn out to be fairer; Soviet Communism did not, though it was clearly undermined by the actions of capitalist businesses and governments). Capitalism has of course spread and evolved over the past 500 years, but its tendency to create imbalances and to favour one set of interests over others has remained constant. If there are certain immutable laws of capitalism which shape the way all economic activity is conducted, there is little hope of improvement. Voluntary restraint would certainly fail, because firms will not unilaterally undertake to curb profitable pursuits in conditions of relentless competition. This leaves regulation, which was mentioned as a possibility in Chapter 4. My guess is that only where pollution or resident hostility becomes so bad that this leads to an exodus of tourists and hence economic decline – in other words only where there is a wide convergence of interests – would governments sign up to it.

For the other point that we have attempted to emphasize in this book is the divergence of interests in the modern world that makes ensuring equitable development so difficult. No development, whether of tourism or of some other activity, will be able to satisfy all the competing interests present within any given community. Here we could learn from the work of the great philosopher Sir Isaiah Berlin. Berlin believed that the myriad ideals, aspirations and values of mankind can never all be compatible, and that 'the necessity of choosing between absolute claims is then an inescapable characteristic of the human condition' (Berlin, 1997: 239). The policy-maker's task is thus not to resolve all differences – it cannot be done – but to accommodate this natural diversity by balancing contradictory claims and making trade-offs. Where tourism is concerned, it would have to be balanced against other industries, its impacts in one sphere weighed against those in another in an attempt to produce the best form of it that would be possible, while accepting that such a form could never be perfect.

In many cases the inevitable trade-offs that tourism development entails have not been made with such care because the balance of power both worldwide and within countries is not even, a situation which has resulted from the spread of capitalism. But given tourism's importance in the post-manufacturing world economy, and the improbability of any other system replacing capitalism in the near future, it seems likely that few destinations will be better off without it.

The future

Prediction is always dangerous. But it seems safe enough to suggest that, since the natural urge to travel is increasingly easy to satisfy, and as holidays can meet so many needs, tourism will not become less important in the future. Not only are the numbers of people travelling forecast to grow over the next twenty years, the numbers of people employed in the tourism industry and the number of countries or regions joining those for whom the industry is already important are also expected to increase. Greater awareness of tourism's negative impacts has done nothing to stop absolute growth, nor to discourage new entrants to the market.

By 2007, worldwide employment in tourism is expected to grow by 46 per cent (Bar-On, 1997). By 2020 the World Tourism Organization is forecasting a threefold growth in international travellers over 1996, estimating that 1.6 billion tourists will be visiting foreign countries annually. Receipts from their travel are expected to exceed $2 trillion (WTO, 1997b). While Germany, the USA, Italy, Japan and the UK will still be among the world's top generating markets by this time, they will have been joined by China (in fourth place) and Russia (in ninth) according to the WTO. Moreover, China, it is predicted, will be the world's top destination (WTO, 1997b).

Certainly, countries such as China and Russia – and South Africa, which in 1996 received three times as many visitors as it did in 1990 (Travel and tourism survey, *The Economist*, 10 January 1998) – offer enormous additional scope both as generating and receiving countries. If they are able to develop successful domestic tourism industries as well as capitalizing on continued interest in long-haul travel – forecast to rise from 18 per cent of all travel in 1995 to 24 per cent by 2020 (WTO, 1997b) – they will thwart suggestions that the world's destinations can no longer accommodate all its tourists. For, despite assertions that the world's tourist destinations are already over-crowded, there are still vast areas that have never seen a tourist. It is possible to envisage a kind of merry-go-round of resorts rising and falling in popularity, as have the English seaside and Spanish costas, at different stages in their lifecycle.

Nevertheless, these figures should be viewed with caution. The WTO has been overoptimistic (or overpessimistic, depending on your point of view) in its forecasts before, failing to anticipate economic recession in the West and caught out by blips following the Gulf war. Of course the organization cannot be expected to be clairvoyant, but given the impact of political and economic events on tourism flows, some acknowledgement that growth is unlikely to proceed exponentially might have been in order.

We can be sure that wars and terrorism will not cease in the near future and that, thanks to the very nature of capitalism, parts of the world are almost bound to experience a recession before 2020. The late 1997 collapse of many Asian economies will have a serious inhibiting effect on the travelling habits of the region's inhabitants. Indeed, the WTTC projected that this would cause more than half a million jobs to be lost in the tourism industry worldwide. And while continuing economic growth and modernization in China does look set to produce the kind of conditions that would encourage and enable its citizens to travel in large numbers, how can we be sure that a regime which has not matched its move towards economic liberalization with any similar political change will permit them to do so?

Political change elsewhere, on the other hand, might also affect numbers and distribution. What, for example, might be the consequences of a continued resurgence of Islamism? Although Islam is not inimical to tourism *per se*, certain types of development and behaviour are likely to be frowned upon (c.f. Aziz, 1995). Ethnic rivalry persists in the Balkans. Supposing it were to spill over into Greece and Turkey? Ethnic refugees could also be joined by migrants fleeing northwards from poverty and famine in the south, if economic disparities continue to widen.This is further evidence for the need to consider both political and economic factors when thinking about the evolution of tourism.

All the same, the coincidence of high growth forecasts with increasing integration of the world economy and the concomitant spread of capitalism does demonstrate how industrialization has predisposed populations towards tourism. If, as we have suggested, there is a human travel imperative, then it is natural that, as more people become economically and politically able to travel, the ranks of tourists will swell. The question for the future is whether their tourism will take the same form, and have the same impacts, as that of their predecessors.

A tourist-generating development cycle

Much has been made of the 'new tourism' (Poon, 1993). Markets have become more segmented, packages more flexible, independent travel more common and tourists more sophisticated. Demographic and social changes in the West are also producing new markets – comfortably-off and fitter pensioners, older single people, child-free (and hence more affluent) gay couples – who are influencing supply. 'Niche' products have grown up in response to demand for alternatives to the beach holiday and at least some tourists have become aware of environmental problems and are avoiding polluted resorts, forcing authorities and tour operators to take action if they want to remain in business. Advances in information technology are facilitating these developments. While the truth of this is evident in the range of specialist holidays now advertised in the press, it is not clear that first-time tourists from new generating countries will necessarily travel in this way, at least to start with.

Although West European tourists are becoming more independent, East Europeans have largely confined themselves to taking package holidays as they have entered the tourism market. There has been a rapid growth in Central and Eastern Europe of travel agents and tour operators offering 1970s-style packages to the Mediterranean (Hall, 1995: 235). In post-apartheid South Africa a new sun, sea and sand market has grown up among the black population, revitalizing a sector of which whites were growing tired (Seaton, 1996a: 359). For cultural as well as economic reasons (group travel perhaps being the first choice for previously heavily collectivized societies), it seems likely that, if and when the Chinese become tourists in any great numbers, they too will have their first experiences on a package tour. In other words, there may be a mass tourism development cycle through which most tourist generating societies have to pass before segmentation and diversification take place (Hall, 1997) (and this cycle may be replicated in some forms of 'new' tourism – see below). Its existence will have implications for the kind of impacts likely to occur or increase as more first-time tourists emerge. On the one hand, there is an opportunity to learn from the environmental and social mistakes of the past; on the other, the need to make short-term profits characteristic of capitalism might encourage such mistakes to be ignored. It is here that the 'sustainable' lobby could most profitably be concentrated.

Containment

If economic trends are going to encourage ever more tourism, are there other developments that might contain or discourage it? We will end by discussing four possibilities: the growth of 'tourism ghettos', which may ultimately include outer space; the impact of global warming; the invention of virtual reality; and Urry's notion that tourism's very ubiquity will cause it to fade away.

Tourism ghettos: old wine in new bottles?

We discussed above the fact that mass tourism has been revitalized in the newer generating countries. Even in the West, however, it is at best 'disappearing' slowly: in the UK in 1994 there was a 40 per cent rise in package holidays over those taken in 1993 thanks to a price war among tour operators. More interestingly, some new or revitalized types of tourism appear to be replicating old patterns in a new product, but in a way that makes them less visible. One such is cruising. In the 1960s the US cruise ship industry was a moribund entity that appealed only to the very rich. It appeared to have lost out irrevocably to the jet engine. In the 1990s, however, it is one of the fastest growing areas of tourism, an achievement that has been made possible only by appealing to mass markets. In addition to changing the way cruises were packaged and distributed (Hobson, 1993), companies began targeting entirely new market segments such as 18–30 year-olds and families with young children. In 1974 Carnival Cruise Lines had entered the market with their 'fun ship' concept (Hobson, 1993). The idea was that the ship should double as an all-inclusive resort, with little attention paid to any ports it might call at, and it proved to be a huge success. Indeed, in some cases, ships have become floating holiday camps with no further destination in mind, but offering a range of organized activities, swimming pools and nightlife.

121

Similar kinds of resort bubbles can also be found on land, in the form of Center Parcs' domed enclosures in Europe, 5,600 square metres of covered 'rain forest' in Nebraska and a Japanese water park offering a roofed-over beach and a surf-filled sea (Travel and tourism survey, *The Economist*, 10 January 1998). Visiting Disney's sites in the USA, Japan and France also constitutes a holiday in itself. In other words, many people are opting to stay in the kinds of artificial holiday centres, or ghettos, advocated by Krippendorf (1987) as a solution to ecological and cultural problems.

Such centres do offer a partial solution to containing tourist numbers, protecting host populations from too much contact and guarding against environmental degradation. Cultural despoliation could also be limited by the craze for simulacra if replicas of vulnerable sites such as the Valley of the Kings and Stonehenge were built. An open-air 'museum' containing copies of some fifty of the world's major natural and human-built wonders is already being built in Shenzhen, China (Hitchcock, Stanley and Siu, 1997). However, tourist ghettos create further problems of their own. Although they may provide employment for local people, they strongly – indeed, totally in the case of fun ships – inhibit the spending of money outside the centre. And while autonomous sites like Disneyland and Center Parcs may be able to deal with the waste they create, cruise ships cannot, adding pollution injury to economic insult for the destinations around which they sail.

Perhaps a more viable way to deal with the problem of future numbers would be to transport tourists off the planet, taking their negative impacts with them (though pollution is created at launch sites). As was discussed in Chapter 10, a sizeable fraction of the public has shown a desire to fly in space and by 2020 it might just be possible. Several tourism companies, in particular the Japanese Shimizu Corporation, have also shown interest. However, the real driving force behind space tourism comes from people in the space community itself, who believe that its development is the only way to ensure cheap access to space for scientific, other commercial and exploratory purposes. The problem is that cheap access will not be assured until the numbers buying space travel reach a similar level to those taking airline flights by the 1960s. This is unlikely to occur until the risks of an accident (currently around one in 280 in the world's safest vehicle, the reusable Space Shuttle) are reduced to the level associated with commercial aviation. The costs and technical difficulties of achieving such a leap in safety may not be considered worthwhile when other operations can be carried out robotically or by trained astronauts aware of the dangers, however, thus creating a vicious circle from which it is hard to escape. Outer space will not solve Earth's tourism problems for years to come.

Global warming

A phenomenon with more likelihood of altering patterns of tourism is that of global warming. In Europe the apparent trend towards warmer summers and milder winters could see summer holidaymakers in the north-west staying at home, other resorts extending their season, but winter sports enthusiasts heading further afield – to North America or even Japan – in an effort to find snow. This could radically alter local economies in the Mediterranean and Alpine regions, not to mention in the Scottish highlands. In the latter two increased summer tourism might make good the loss; the Mediterranean countries would have to pursue the winter sun market. In addition, if preventive measures are not taken, rising sea levels could wipe Venice right off the tourism map and inundate some of the Pacific and Indian Ocean islands. Since many of these are currently highly dependent on tourism, devastating environmental effects would have an equally devastating economic impact. Drought, desertification and a greater risk of forest fire in other parts of the world, as well as flash-flooding in yet others – indeed, greater climatic instability generally – could also make tourism less viable. How far tourism is affected overall will depend on global scientific efforts and political will to arrest climate change and mitigate its consequences, as well as on how far changes in the weather have been correctly interpreted, but if some densely populated areas are stricken, supranational regulation of tourist numbers (among other things) may be required and accepted, as limits on chlorofluorocarbon use have been – albeit grudgingly – in the case of ozone depletion. Such an occurrence could point the way to a more general acknowledgement by the tourism industry that certain forms of legislation may be in everyone's best interests.

Virtual reality

If global warming does put major tourism destinations out of bounds, 'virtual tourism' might come into its own. Tourists would use a headset and computer to enter a three-dimensional virtual reality (VR) world of sound, vision and a limited sense of touch. Currently such worlds are less than convincing but we are assured that the technology to make VR more real and less virtual – with the inclusion of smells and tastes for example – will soon be available.

Using VR could be another way to keep people away from vulnerable sites like Venice, Everest or wetland areas. Advocates point out that, since virtual holidays can be had without queues, delayed flights, submission to bad weather, harrassment, crime or accidents at the destination, and since they could bring inaccessible or expensive 'locations' such as the Amazon, the Sahara or the celebrity island of Mustique into one's living room, they may ultimately be preferred to the real thing. As with tourism ghettos or the Shenzhen museum, however, this would be a mixed blessing. While the environmental impacts of tourism would be greatly reduced by VR, it would wipe out the beneficial economic impacts for destinations. One could almost imagine a situation where the latter might try to 'copyright' their reality in order to avoid the greatest leakage of all.

All the same it seems unlikely that many people will choose virtual holidays unless the Earth's climate becomes so upset that there is no alternative – in which case basic survival is likely to be uppermost in people's minds. No one is going to spend a fortnight in front of a computer screen – when would you eat? – so immersion would have to take place at selected intervals, after which the home environment would again intrude. The sense of being away would be much more temporary. Virtual reality could certainly provide a means for people such as the frail elderly, the sick and disabled, people who are unable physically to travel, to experience far away destinations vicariously, perhaps courtesy of their health services. It could also be used by those on low incomes as the technology is likely to be cheaper than a holiday. But for others it is more likely to provide a spur to the 'real' thing.

Indeed, this is how it will most commonly be used – as a marketing tool giving the customer a taste of trips to come. If exploited in this way by the tourism industry, VR could actually act to increase the numbers of people travelling: as more have access to the sights and sounds of remote locations, more may be inclined to visit them in person – and take their friends along. For another disadvantage of VR is that, at least at the moment, it can only be experienced individually, while a key element of tourism is that it should involve time with other people. Who wants to laze on palm-fringed shores alone? The people problem is just as important where business tourism is concerned. Despite being heralded as a break-through when it emerged in the 1970s, 'teleconferencing' has never really taken off and shows no signs of threatening the conference market. Business travellers may complain that there is nothing glamorous about jetlag and always being on the move, but in the main they still prefer face-to-face, in-the-flesh interaction – as well as the opportunity to get away from the office – and no amount of technology looks likely to change this. (Instead, hotels are putting more and more effort into making their business rooms more like home.)

A postmodern end to tourism?

On this basis it seems unlikely that people will ultimately prefer to 'access' their leisure through the video screen, leading to the 'end of tourism' as we know it. Nevertheless, this is what has been posited by Urry (1995) and other commentators on the postmodern. The suggestion is that, as tourism has become 'de-differentiated' from other aspects of life, such as work, shopping and (arguably) urban culture; because it is so concerned with cultural production and hence the new service economy, rather than with manufactures; and as everyone is either a tourist or an object of tourism – by being consciously or unconsciously on display to tourists – the phenomenon will, by being everywhere, also be nowhere.

The trouble with this point of view is that it assumes that undoubted changes in the pattern of tourism are universal. But, as we have seen, large numbers of people are still taking old-style holidays and more seem set to do so. Moreover, postmodernism is at best a patchy phenomenon whose effects are not uniform. It may be correct to speak of the USA as a postmodern society but it is less so to attach the epithet to Ireland or Portugal. Even within so-called postmodern societies there are differences: California is rather more postmodern than Wyoming, for instance, and London more so than mid-Wales. To many people, postmodernism must seem a complete irrelevance. Technological changes, post-industrialization and globalization have affected some lives not by giving them greater choice and flexibility but by depriving them of work, livelihood and identity, leading to a continuing and seemingly unbreachable polarization between the haves and have-nots. Around 40 per cent of the UK population still does not take a holiday, a figure that has hardly changed in the last ten or twenty years, which means that the good as well as the bad impacts of tourism are not equally shared. On the other hand, technological change has also given rise to a category of 'don't wants' – people who reject the depersonalizing aspects of the new information revolution in favour of continued human interaction.

Finally, we are also witnessing a backlash against aspects of postmodernism that may yet reverse some of the trends that have made tourism so ubiquitous. The individualism that has reached its apotheosis under late capitalism is now being attacked through the advocacy of movements such as communitarianism, an attempt to blend socialist ideas of the common good with individual responsibility. Attacks against the 'dumbing down' of society, with its three-minute culture and obsession with surface are also proliferating. Some of them may be misguided but they do demonstrate concern over the loss of absolute values. Most damagingly, parallels have been drawn between postmodernism and fascism – and few like to be called a fascist. But, according to MacCannell (1992: 187), the similarities are too obvious to ignore:

> The attack on the notion of truth as so much metaphysical baggage, the sense of living in an infinite instant at the end of history, nostalgia for the folk-primitive-peasant, schizophrenia at the level of culture, and general ennui periodically interrupted by euphoric release from all constraint. All these are named characteristics of both classic fascism and postmodern aesthetics.

MacCannell conveniently disregards the rigid hierarchies and subordination of the individual to the will of the state that are also commonly associated with fascism but do not bear much resemblance to postmodern realities. But he may be right in implying that both arise at times of uncertainty and confusion. Certainly the changes wrought by post-industrialization have given rise to much confusion.

Even so, I do not think the urge to travel will disappear in the near or even longer-term future. People are not confused about the general desire to travel. Indeed, it can be a means of temporarily escaping confusion. It is an urge that has been present for millennia and for many people it has been made realizable for the first time by current economic and political circumstances. It follows then that the patterns of international tourism will only change if economic and political conditions are altered. It seems likely that there will be an increase in piecemeal attempts to stave off the negative impacts of tourism, through legislation (or possibly pricing) limiting numbers at certain sites and through the creation of copies. But unless there is a radical change in the global political economy, leading to an entirely new set of social relations, the likelihood of any fundamental alteration in the practice of tourism seems slim.

Bibliography

Akama, J. S. (1997). Tourism development in Kenya: problems and policy alternatives. *Progress in Tourism and Hospitality Research*, **3**, 95–105.

Anon. (1997) Nature groups work with junta in Burma's ethnic killing fields. *Observer*, 23 March.

Anon (1998). Airtours margins hit as tourists avoid Middle East. *Independent*, 19 February.

Archer, B. and Cooper, C. (1994). The positive and negative aspects of tourism. In *Global Tourism: The Next Decade* (W. Theobald, ed.) pp. 73–91, Butterworth-Heinemann.

Archer, B. and Fletcher, J. (1996). The economic impact of tourism in the Seychelles. *Annals of Tourism Research*, **23**, 32–47.

Avella, A. E. and Mills, A. S. (1996). Tourism in Cuba in the 1990s: back to the future? *Tourism Management*, **17**, 55–60.

Aziz, H. (1995). Understanding attacks on tourists in Egypt. *Tourism Management*, **16**, 91–95.

Balmer, J. (1996). *Classical Women Poets*. Bloodaxe.

Bar-On, R. (1997). Databank: Europe. *Tourism Economics*, **3**, 399–411.

Becheri, E. (1991). Rimini and co – the end of a legend? Dealing with the algae effect. *Tourism Management*, **12**, 229–35.

Bender, B. and Edmonds, M. (1992). Stonehenge: whose past? What past? *Tourism Management*, **13**, 355–57.

Berlin, I. (1997). Two concepts of liberty. In *The Proper Study of Mankind*, (H. Hardy and R. Hausheer, eds) pp. 191– 242, Chatto & Windus.

Binyon, M. (1997). Nile town counts cost of massacre. *The Times*, 31 December.

Boniface, P. (1997). Behind the scenes: the tourism periphery to France's Mediterranean coast. Paper presented to the Peripheral Area Tourism conference, Bornholm, September.

Boorstin, D. (1964). *The Image: A Guide to Pseudo-Events in America.* Harper & Row.

Borg, J. van der, Costa, P. and Gotti, G. (1996). Tourism in European heritage cities. *Annals of Tourism Research*, **23**, 306–21.

Breathnach, P., Henry, M., Drea, S. and O'Flaherty, M. (1994). Gender in Irish tourism employment. In *Tourism: A Gender Analysis* (V. Kinnaird and D. Hall, eds) pp. 52–73, Wiley.

Britton, S. G. (1982). The political economy of tourism in the Third World. *Annals of Tourism Research*, **9**, 331–58.

Bryden, J. (1973). *Tourism and Development: A Case Study of the Commonwealth Caribbean.* Cambridge University Press.

Burkart, J. (1988). Letter to the editor. Tourism: a vital force for peace. *Tourism Management*, **9**, 254.

Burkart, J. and Medlik, S. (1981). *Tourism: Past, Present and Future.* Butterworth-Heinemann.

Burns, P. and Holden, A. (1995). *Tourism: A New Perspective.* Prentice Hall.

Butler, R. W. (1980). The concept of a tourist area cycle of evolution: implications for management of resources. *Canadian Geographer*, **24**, 5–12.

Butler, R. (1992). Alternative tourism: the thin edge of the wedge. In *Tourism Alternatives* (V. L. Smith and W. R. Eadington, eds) pp. 31–46, Wiley.

Bystrzanowski, J., ed. (1989). *Tourism as a Factor of Change: A Sociocultural Study.* Centre for Research and Documentation in the Social Sciences, Vienna.

Calder, S. (1997). Is it safe to travel along the Nile? If you're careful .... *Independent*, 19 September.

Carmichael, B., Peppard, D. M. Jr and Boudreau, F. A. (1996). Megaresort on my doorstep: local resident attitudes toward Foxwood casino and casino gambling on nearby Indian reservation land. *Journal of Travel Research*, **34**, 9–16.

Carruthers, D. V. (1996). Indigenous ecology and the politics of linkage in Mexican social movements. *Third World Quarterly*, **17**, 1007–28.

Cater, E. (1993). Ecotourism in the Third World: problems for sustainable tourism development. *Tourism Management*, **14**, 85–90.

Clarke, I. F. (1988). To the uttermost ends of the Earth. *Tourism Management*, **9**, 171–5.

Cohen, E. (1988). Authenticity and commoditization in tourism. *Annals of Tourism Research*, **15**, 371–86.

Crick, M. (1988). Sun, sex, sights, savings and servility. *Criticism, Heresy and Interpretation*, **1**, 37–76.

Cukier, J. and Wall, G. (1994). Informal tourism employment: vendors in Bali, Indonesia. *Tourism Management*, **15**, 464–7.

D'Amour, L. J. (1992). Promoting sustainable tourism – the Canadian approach. *Tourism Management*, **13**, 258–62.

Dann, G. (1996). *The Language of Tourism: A Sociolinguistic Perspective.* CAB International.

Davidson, J. (1997). High hopes for the people. *Scotland on Sunday*, 16 November.

Donnelly, P. (1987). Creating national parks – 'a grand, good thing'? *Tourism Management*, **8**, 349–51.

Dupas, A. (1997). *L'Age des Satellites.* Hachette.

Eadington, W. R. and Redman, M. (1991). Economics and tourism. *Annals of Tourism Research*, **18**, 41–56.

Easton, A. (1997). Eco-tourists take classes in jungle survival. *Guardian*, 17 November.

Eber, S. (1992). *Beyond the Green Horizon.* WWF/Tourism Concern.

Elliott, J. (1997). *Tourism: Politics and Public Sector Management.* Routledge.

Enloe, C. (1990). *Bananas, Beaches and Bases: Making Feminist Sense of International Politics.* University of California Press.

Erisman, H. M. (1983). Tourism and cultural dependency in the West Indies. *Annals of Tourism Research*, **10**, 337–61.

Fairbairn-Dunlop, P. (1994). Gender, culture and tourism development in Western Samoa. In *Tourism: A Gender Analysis* (V. Kinnaird and D. Hall, eds) pp. 121–41, Wiley.

Falco, M. (1996). US drug policy: addicted to failure. *Foreign Policy*, **102**, 120–33.

Finney, B. R. (1985a). The prince and the eunuch. In *Interstellar Migration and the Human Experience* (B.R. Finney and E.M. Jones, eds) pp. 196–209, University of California Press.

Finney, B. R. (1985b). Voyagers into ocean space. In *Interstellar Migration and the Human Experience* (B.R. Finney and E.M. Jones, eds) pp. 164–179, University of California Press.

Fisk, R. (1997). Building a new Lebanon ravishes its Ottoman treasures. *Independent*, 26 November.

Frank, A. G. (1967). *Capitalism and Underdevelopment in Latin America. Historical Studies of Chile and Brazil.* Monthly Review Press.

Frank, A. G. (1991). The underdevelopment of development. *Scandinavian Journal of Development Alternatives*, **10**, 48 ff.

Garcia-Ramon, M. D., Canoves, G. and Valdovinos, N. (1995). Farm tourism, gender and the environment in Spain, *Annals of Tourism Research*, **22**, 267–82.

Gilpin, R. (1987). *The Political Economy of International Relations*. Princeton University Press.

Goldenberg, S. (1997). Burma's military turns on itself as economy sinks. *Guardian*, 22 December.

Goodale, T. and Godbey, G. (1988). *The Evolution of Leisure*. Venture Publishing.

Grant, D. (1996). The Package Travel Regulations 1992: damp squib or triumph of self-regulation? *Tourism Management*, **17**, 319–21.

Greenwood, D. (1977/1989). Culture by the pound: an anthropological perspective on tourism as cultural commoditization. In *Hosts and Guests* (V. L. Smith, ed.) pp. 171–85, University of Pennsylvania Press.

Hall, C. M. (1994). *Tourism and Politics: Policy, Power and Place*. Wiley.

Hall, D. R. (1991). Evolutionary pattern of tourism development in Eastern Europe and the Soviet Union. In *Tourism and Economic Development in Eastern Europe and the Soviet Union* (D. R. Hall, ed.) pp. 79–115, Belhaven.

Hall, D. R. (1992). Tourism development in Cuba. In *Tourism and the Less Developed Countries* (D. Harrison, ed.) pp. 102–20, Wiley.

Hall, D. R. (1995). Tourism change in Central and Eastern Europe. In *European Tourism: Regions, Spaces and Restructuring* (A. Montanari and A. M. Williams, eds) pp. 221–44, Wiley.

Hall, D. R. (1997). Tourism prospects in the Balkans. Paper presented to the European Tourism conference, Royal Geographical Society, London, October.

Hall, D. R. and Brown, F. (1996). Towards a welfare focus for tourism research. *Progress in Tourism and Hospitality Research*, **2**, 41–57.

Hall, D. and Kinnaird, V. (1994). A note on women travellers. In *Tourism: A Gender Analysis*, (V. Kinnaird and D. Hall, eds) pp. 188–209, Wiley.

Handszuh, H. (1992). Trade in tourism services under the Uruguay Round. *Tourism Management*, **13**, 263–66.

Harrison, D. (1992). *Tourism in the Less Developed Countries*. Wiley.

Harrison, D. (1994). Tourism and prostitution: sleeping with the enemy? *Tourism Management*, **15**, 435–43.

Hawkins, R. (1994). Putting research into practice – the WTTERC. *Tourism Management*, **15**, 299–301.

Hennessy, S. (1994). Female employment in tourism development in South-west England. In *Tourism: A Gender Analysis* (V. Kinnaird and D. Hall, eds) pp. 35–51.

Hewison, R. (1987). *The Heritage Industry: Britain in a Climate of Decline.* Methuen.

Hillaby, J. (1968). *Journey through Britain.* Constable.

Hinch, T. (1990). Cuban tourism industry – its re-emergence and future. *Tourism Management,* **11,** 214–26.

Hirst, P. and Thompson, G. (1996). *Globalization in Question: The International Economy and the Possibilities of Governance.* Polity.

Hitchcock, M., Stanley, N. and Siu, K. C. (1997). The South-east Asian 'living museum' and its antecedents. In *Tourists and Tourism: Indentifying with People and Places* (S. Abram, J. Waldren and D. V. L. Macleod, eds) pp. 197–221, Berg.

Hobson, J. S. P. (1993). Analysis of the US cruise line industry. *Tourism Management,* **14,** 453–62.

Hobson, J. S. P. (1995). Hong Kong: the transition to 1997. *Tourism Management,* **16,** 15–20.

Hoskin, J. (1984). *Ten Contemporary Thai Artists.* Graphis.

Hughes, G. S. (1995). Authenticity in tourism. *Annals of Tourism Research.* **22,** 781–803.

Hughes, H. L. (1991). Holidays and the economically disadvantaged. *Tourism Management,* **12,** 193–6.

Hunter, C. (1997). Sustainable tourism as an adaptive paradigm. *Annals of Tourism Research,* **24,** 850–67.

Jafari, J. (1987). Tourism models: the sociocultural aspects. *Tourism Management,* **8,** 151–9.

Jafari, J. (1989). An English language literature review. In *Tourism as a Factor of Change: A Sociocultural Study* (J. Bystrzanowski, ed.) pp. 17–60, Centre for Research and Documentation in the Social Sciences, Vienna.

Johnston, L. (1997) Barred from animals' kingdom. *Observer,* 6 April.

Jones, R. J. B. (1995). *Globalisation and Interdependence in the International Political Economy: Rhetoric and Reality.* Pinter.

Kadt, E. de (1979). *Tourism: Passport to Development?* Oxford University Press.

Kohn, T. (1997). Island involvement and the evolving tourist. In *Tourists and Tourism: Identifying with People and Places* (S. Abram, J. Waldren and D. V. L. MacLeod, eds) pp. 13–28, Berg.

Kosters, M. (1984). The deficiencies of tourism science without political science: comment on Richter. *Annals of Tourism Research,* **11,** 610–12.

Krippendorf, J. (1987). *The Holiday Makers: Understanding the Impact of Leisure and Travel.* Butterworth-Heinemann.

Lanfant, M.-F. (1980). Tourism in the process of internationalization. *International Social Science Journal,* **32,** 14–43.

Lanfant, M.-F. and Graburn, N. (1992). International tourism reconsidered: the principle of the alternative. In *Tourism Alternatives* (V. L. Smith and W. R. Eadington, eds) pp. 88–112, Wiley.

Leiper, N. (1979). The framework of tourism: towards a definition of tourism, tourist, and the tourism industry, *Annals of Tourism Research*, **6**, 390–407.

Leiper, N. (1990). *Tourism Systems: An Interdisciplinary Perspective, Department of Management Systems*, Massey University.

Leys, C. (1996). The crisis in 'development theory'. *New Political Economy*, **1**, 41–58.

Lickorish, L. J. (1997). Tourism statistics – the slow move forward. *Tourism Management*, **18**, 491–7.

Long, P. (1995). Casino gambling in the United States: 1994 status and implications. *Tourism Management*, **16**, 189–97.

Loveluck, P. (1989). Report on the Welsh case study for the Vienna Centre's research on tourism as a factor of change, presented to the conference on Tourism and Cultural Change organized by the European Centre for Traditional and Regional Cultures, Llangollen, Wales, September.

M'Nayr, J. (1797). *A Guide from Glasgow, to Some of the Most Remarkable Scenes in the Highlands of Scotland, and to the Falls of the Clyde*. Courier Office, Glasgow.

MacCannell, D. (1976). *The Tourist: A New Theory of the Leisure Class*. Schocken Books.

MacCannell, D. (1992). *Empty Meeting Grounds*. Routledge.

Marshall, D. D. (1996). National development and the globalization discourse: confronting 'imperative' and 'convergence' notions. *Third World Quarterly*, **17**, 875–902.

Maslow, A. (1943). A theory of human motivation. *Psycholgical Review*, **50**, 399–419.

Mathews, H. G. (1975). International tourism and political science research. *Annals of Tourism Research*, **2**, 195–203.

Mathiesen, A. and Wall, G. (1982). *Tourism: Economic, Physical and Social Impacts*. Longman.

May, V. (1995). Environmental implications of the 1992 Winter Olympic Games. *Tourism Management*, **16**, 269–76.

McKercher, B. (1992). Tourism as a conflicting land use. *Annals of Tourism Research*, **19**, 467–81.

McLean, J. (1981). Political theory, international theory and problems of ideology. *Millennium*, **10**, 102–25.

Middleton, V. T. C. (1991). Whither the package tour? *Tourism Management*, **12**, 185–92.

Momsen, J. H. (1994). Tourism, gender and development in the Caribbean. In *Tourism: A Gender Analysis* (V. Kinnaird and D. Hall, eds) pp. 106–20, Wiley.

Morgan, M. (1991). Dressing up to survive – marketing Majorca anew. *Tourism Management*, **12**, 15–20.

Murray, J. and McGinnety, P. (1997). Hong Kong loses its eastern promise. *Scotland on Sunday*, 30 November.

Norfolk, D. (1994). Holidays in hell. *Business Traveller*, **19**, 19.

Noronha, F. (1994). Trouble in paradise: an update on Goa. *The Eye*, **11**, 44–5.

Oberreit, J. (1996). Destruction and reconstruction: the case of Dubrovnik. In *Reconstructing the Balkans: A Geography of the New Southeast Europe* (D. Hall and D. Danta, eds) pp. 67–78, Wiley.

O'Neill, M. A. and Fitz, F. (1996). Northern Ireland tourism: what chance now? *Tourism Management*, **17**, 161–3.

Oppitz, W. (1997). Address to the 10th European Leisure and Recreation Association conference, Dubrovnik, October.

Parfitt, T. (1997). Europe's Mediterranean designs: an analysis of the Euromed relationship with special reference to Egypt. *Third World Quarterly*, **18**, 865–82.

Pattullo, P. (1996). *Last Resorts. The Cost of Tourism in the Caribbean.* Cassell.

Pearce, D. (1995). CER, trans-Tasman tourism and a single aviation market. *Tourism Management*, **16**, 111–20.

Polunin, I. (1989). Japanese travel boom. *Tourism Management*, **10**, 4–8.

Poon, A. (1993). *Tourism, Technology and Competitive Strategies.* CAB International.

Poulsen, T. M. (1977). Migration on the Adriatic coast: some processes associated with the development of tourism. In *Population and Migration Trends in Eastern Europe* (H. L. Kostanick, ed.) pp. 197–215, Westview Press.

Pryer, M. (1997). The traveller as a destination pioneer. *Progress in Tourism and Hospitality Research*, **3**, 225–37.

Pyne, S. (1988). Space: a third Great Age of Discovery. *Space Policy*, **3**, 187–99.

Richter, L. K. (1983). Tourism politics and political science: a case of not so benign neglect. *Annals of Tourism Research*, **10**, 313–35.

Richter, L. K. (1984). A search for missing answers to questions never asked: reply to Kosters. *Annals of Tourism Research*, **11**, 613–15.

Richter, L. K. (1989). *The Politics of Tourism in Asia.* University of Hawaii Press.

Richter, L. K. and Waugh, W. L. Jr (1991). Terrorism and tourism as logical companions. In *Managing Tourism* (S. Medlik, ed.) pp. 318–26, Butterworth-Heinemann.

Roberts, M. (1998). Travel and tourism survey. *The Economist*, 10 January.

Rodriguez, M. and Portales, J. (1994). Tourism and NAFTA: towards a regional tourism policy. *Tourism Management*, **15**, 319–22.

Ryan, C. (1997). Similar motivations – diverse behaviours. In *The Tourist Experience: A New Introduction* (C. Ryan, ed.) pp. 25–47, Cassell.

Saglio, C. (1979). Tourism for discovery: a project in Lower Casamance, Senegal. In *Tourism: Passport to Development?* (E. de Kadt, ed.) pp. 321–35, Oxford University Press.

Said, E. (1978). *Orientalism*. Routledge & Kegan Paul.

Schiller, H. (1976). *Communication and Cultural Dominance*. International Arts and Sciences Press.

Seaton, A. V. (1996a). Destination marketing. In *Marketing Tourism Products: Concepts, Issues, Cases* (A. V. Seaton and M. M. Bennett, eds) pp. 350–76, Thomson Business Press.

Seaton, A. V. (1996b). Tourism history in Scotland: approaches, sources and issues. Mimeo.

Seaton, A. V. (1997). Demonstration effects or relative deprivation? The counter-revolutionary pressures of tourism in Cuba. *Progress in Tourism and Hospitality Research*, **3**, 307–20.

Sharpley, R. (1994). *Tourism, Tourists and Society*. Elm Publications.

Sharpley, R., Sharpley, J. and Adams, J. (1996). Travel advice or trade embargo? The impacts and implications of official travel advice. *Tourism Management*, **17**, 1–8.

Shivji, I. G. (1973). *Tourism and Socialist Development*. Tanzania Publishing House.

Smith, G. (1994). Implications of the North American Free Trade Agreement for the US tourism industry. *Tourism Management*, **15**, 323–6.

Smith, V. (1992). Boracay, Phillipines: a case study in 'alternative' tourism. In *Tourism Alternatives* (V. L. Smith and W. R. Eadington, eds) pp. 135–57, Wiley.

Soo Ann, L. (1973). Tourism builds a smokeless economic base. *Proceedings of the Pacific Area Travel Association*, Kyoto, Japan, 207–9.

Teuscher, H. (1993). Swiss travel saving fund. *Tourism Management*, **4**, 216–19.

Towner, J. (1995). What is tourism's history? *Tourism Management*, **16**, 339–43.

Towner, J. (1996). *An Historical Geography of Recreation and Tourism in the Western World*. Wiley.

Townsend, A. R. (1997). *Making a Living in Europe*, pp. 172–90, Routledge.

Tucker, H. (1997). The ideal village: interactions through tourism in Central Anatolia. In *Tourists and Tourism: Identifying with People and Places* (S. Abram, J. Waldren and D. V. L. MacLeod, eds) pp. 107–28, Berg.

Turner, L. and Ash, J. (1975). *The Golden Hordes*. Constable.

Urry, J. (1990). *The Tourist Gaze*. Sage.

Urry, J. (1995). *Consuming Places*. Routledge.

Vellas, F. and Becherel, L. (1995). *International Tourism*. Macmillan.

Vulliamy, E. (1997). Blazing battle to keep the West wild. *Observer*, 12 October.

Wager, J. (1995). Developing a strategy for the Angkor World Heritage Site. *Tourism Management*, **16**, 515–23.

Wall, G. (1996). Rethinking impacts of tourism. *Progress in Tourism and Hospitality Research*, **2**, 207–15.

Wallerstein, I. (1974). *The Modern World-System: Capitalist Agriculture and the Origins of the European World-Economy in the Sixteenth Century*. Academic Press.

Waters, M. (1995). *Globalization*. Routledge.

Wheeller, B. (1991). Tourism's troubled times. *Tourism Management*, **12**, 91–6.

Wheeller, B. (1993). Sustaining the ego. *Journal of Sustainable Tourism*, **1**, 121–9.

Wilden, A. (1987). *Man and Woman, War and Peace: The Strategist's Companion*. Routledge & Kegan Paul.

Wilson, D. (1997). Paradoxes of tourism in Goa. *Annals of Tourism Research*, **24**, 52–75.

Wilton, A. and Bignamini, I. (1996). *Grand Tour: The Lure of Italy in the Eighteenth Century*. Tate Gallery Publishing.

Witt, S. (1991). Tourism in Cyprus – balancing the benefits and costs. *Tourism Management*, **12**, 37–46.

Wood, E. M. (1981). The separation of the economic and political in capitalism. *New Left Review*, **127**, 64–95.

Wood, R. C. (1996). The last feather-bedded industry? Government, politics and the hospitality industry during and after the 1992 General Election. *Tourism Management*, **17**, 583–92.

WTO (1981). Manila Declaration. World Tourism Organization.

WTO (1997a). *Yearbook of Tourism Statistics*, vol. 1. World Tourism Organization.

WTO (1997b). *Tourism: 2020 Vision*. World Tourism Organization.

WTTC (1990). Press release. Quoted in 'Monitor', *Tourism Management*, **11**, 183.

WTTC (1991). Press release. Quoted in 'Monitor', *Tourism Management*, **12**, 269.

Young, G. (1973). *Tourism: Blessing or Blight?* Penguin.

Index

Printed in the United Kingdom
by Lightning Source UK Ltd.
101332UKS00001B/392